EXPOSED

THE BUSINESS OF PHOTOGRAPHY

Deryck van Steenderen

Published by

VERSE CREATIVE

Published by Verse Creative

www.versecreative.co.za

Eighth Edition published September 2016

First published October 2013

ISBN 978-0-9921992-4-1

DISCLAIMER - PLEASE NOTE

This book is written and published for informational purposes only. Neither the Publisher nor the Author is engaged in rendering professional advice or services to the individual reader. The ideas, procedures and suggestions contained in this book are not intended as a substitute for consulting with legal, financial or other professional advisors. The onus is on you to check the accuracy and legitimacy of the information in this book before applying it.

Use of this book is at your own risk. Neither the Author nor the Publisher shall be liable for any loss or damage allegedly arising from any information or suggestion in this book.

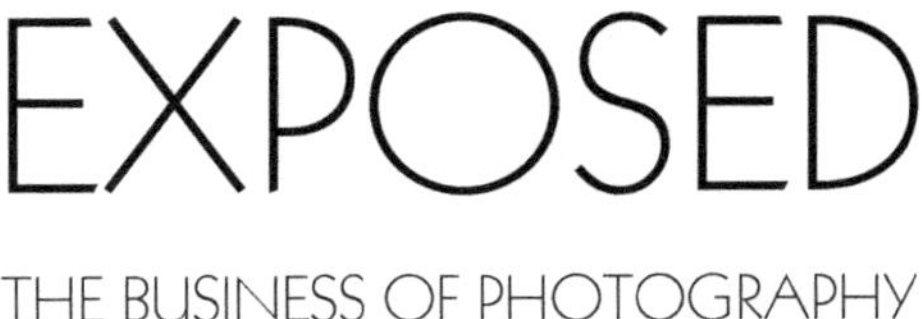

THE BUSINESS OF PHOTOGRAPHY

Deryck van Steenderen

Published by

VERSE CREATIVE

"In response to those who say to
stop dreaming and face reality, I say
keep dreaming and make reality."

Judah Isvaran

"I am so impressed with your new book Deryck! A good spread of practical information in the chapters. An amazing amount of work to have contributed to the South African professional photo community. We all owe you! Well done and thank you."

- Mike Hall, Commercial Photographer

"Just read the best photography business book I have ever seen, not just in SA, but anywhere! Well done."

- Corné van Driel, Commercial Photographer

INTRODUCTION

This is the book I wish I could have read when I was starting out as a young photographer. I borrowed an established commercial photographer's studio to shoot my first fashion test shoot in at the age of 19. I was fired up and felt like I could conquer the world. His advice? *"Choose another career, you can always do this as a hobby."*

At the time I thought he was just being negative but many years later I now understand what he meant.

Photography is a beautiful art form. Since it's inception in 1790 the art and science of photography has blossomed into a massive global industry worth billions of dollars every year.

Most photographers are artists and are drawn to photography as a career to pursue their passion for their medium. Very few are prepared for the reality of the industry.

Whilst honing our technical and creative skills as a photographer we also need to hone our business skills, without which we are unlikely to succeed as professional photographers.

Our goal should be to have a financially viable, sustainable career producing the best work possible as professional photographers. A financially viable and sustainable career means one in which we are able to draw a market related salary every month, with standard employment benefits such as annual and sick leave, whilst making provision for our retirement and paying our bills on time. Just as every other career deems this normal, so should we.

I welcome your constructive feedback on this book. It's not perfect but it is a labour of love. I'm not an attorney, nor an accountant. I'm a photographer who's learnt a few things along the way and will update this book from time to time. *Please check the supporting website www.exposed.co.za from time to time for updates and revisions.*

My gratitude goes to my family, LBS Margaret, Pierre, Lynne, Mick and my Dad for your support over the years. Thank you. MBMLMS Bronwen thank you for your encouragement and support and for believing in me when I doubted myself. To the photographers I assisted who taught me so much, especially Mike Hall, Dirk Pieters, Tim Petersen, Dan Holmqvist and Oliver Lwowski, thank you for sharing your knowledge and equipment so freely with me.

To my first clients who believed in me, especially Dawn Schlunz of Associated Magazines, Lynne Wilson of the HSRC, Nadine Thompson of New Media Publishers, Imogen Pretorius and Haneem Majiet-Abader of New Highway Publishers and Lesley Price of The Publishing Partnership, thank you. To my clients who followed, especially Skip Margetts (the best producer I've ever worked with), Chenel Ferreira-Lotz, Nina Phillips, Mila Crewe-Brown, Jane Eager, Marie Esterhuyse, Sabina Jakub, Nina Daniel-Gruber, Liesl Nicholson, Juan Geel, Wendy Clegg and Natasha Johnson, thank you for choosing me.

To the teams I've worked with, thank you.

Andrew Pittaway, thank you for your foresight and courage and for trying so valiantly to herd cats. Geof Kirby, for thanklessly campaigning for our rights, thank you. John Spicer of Dr. Gernholtz Inc. and Dr. Owen Dean of Spoor & Fisher, Professor at the University of Stellenbosch and incumbent of the Anton Mostert Chair of Intellectual Property Law, thank you for your advice on Intellectual Property Law and sharing your knowledge with the photographic community at large.

Thank you to all of you, I couldn't have done it without you.

This book is my part in making the world a better place, one image at a time.

Deryck van Steenderen
Professional Photographer
www.deryckvs.com

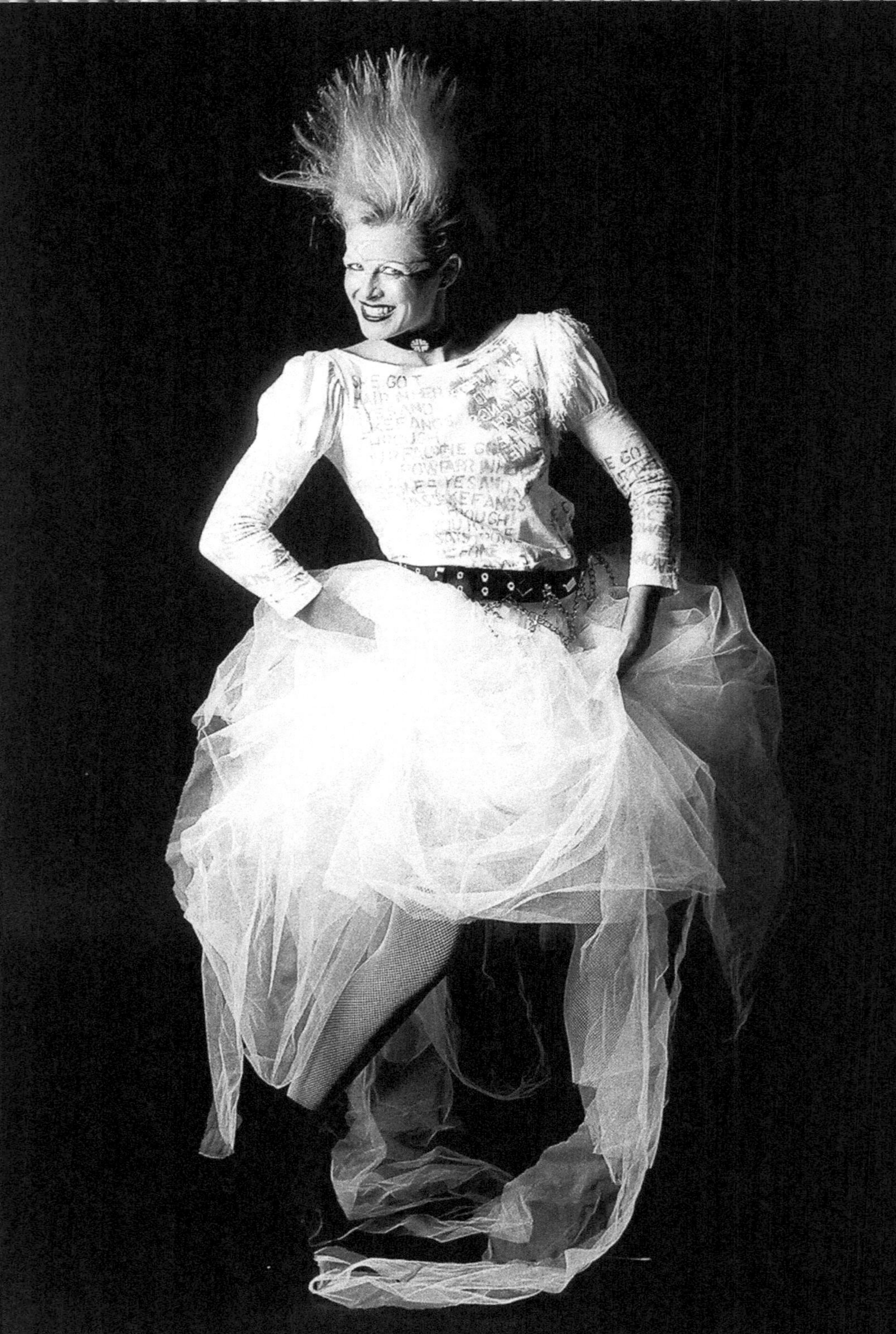

CHAPTER 1

SO YOU WANT TO BE A ROCKSTAR?

"Creativity is being able to see what everyone has seen and think what nobody else has thought so that you can do what nobody else has done."

John C. Maxwell

Many people are drawn to photography through their love of creating beautiful images. As their skill level improves the inevitable question arises, "Can I make a living from this?" Whilst photography can be an excellent way to supplement your existing income becoming a professional photographer is a little more challenging.

Professional photography quite simply means photography from which a photographer makes their living or derives their main source of income from. It is not indicative of the level or quality of the photographer's work, merely that the photographer earns a living from it.

It is essential to establish two principles from the beginning:

1. Professional photography is a business
2. Businesses exist to make a profit

The salary that you draw from your photography business is your reward for your time invested into your business. Just as an employee of any other business is entitled to draw a salary, have paid annual and sick leave, have a pension/provident fund and have a medical aid, so are you.

The fundamental difference between an employee and a business owner is that the business owner carries the risk, responsibility and liability of the business failing. Profit is the reward for that risk. As a professional photographer, regardless of whether you trade as a Sole Proprietor or a registered Company, your business goal is to make a profit to reward yourself for the risk you are taking being in business. It is never good enough to work for break-even. Without profit you are unlikely to be able to build up working capital reserves that you will need for rainy days, both for your business and yourself.

Photography is a business worth billions of dollars globally. Like all other well run businesses your starting point for determining how much you should charge is in calculating how much it costs you to run your business.

Apart from the actual costs of running your business you also need to build up a working capital reserve, or 'oh shit fund'. Whilst planning helps to reduce the effects of the curve balls life throws at you it's impossible to predict every one.

The digital explosion took place and within a few years we no longer shot film for commercial clients. This meant that we had to buy new, very expensive digital equipment. My equipment overheads were five times what they had been, with clients forcing our rates to remain the same. In the beginning I focussed on buying the best lenses and hired the camera bodies. My thinking was that digital cameras are essentially computers and would be out of date quickly. I did this while waiting for the quality of digital images to catch up to the quality of film. Many photographers jumped in straight away buying cameras that were sold for two-thirds of the price new a year later. Most of them were unable to recover their investment they made in their camera before having to replace it. Their cameras were worth a fraction of the cost second hand and they made substantial losses on their equipment. I call this the 'digital dilemma'. Whilst shooting film, film technology improved all the time. Grain was finer and colour accuracy and saturation improved. This meant that you could shoot on the same camera system for years as long as you bought the best film on the market. The problem with digital photography is that the improvements are in the sensor itself. Because of the way the cameras are made we are unable to replace the sensor when a better one is released, forcing us to buy new cameras. This loads our overheads, making photography less financially viable than before.

The 'global economic downturn' caused by reckless, greedy executives who cared more about self enrichment than peoples well being, destroyed the photographic market. Within three years eight magazines that I shot for closed down. Advertising budgets were slashed globally and widespread retrenchments took place. The bottom fell out of the market. Photographers all around me were selling their equipment, and in some cases their homes, in an attempt to pay their expenses, many closing their businesses altogether. Four years later clients still use the economy to plead poverty, many of them whilst declaring healthy profits. Many magazines barely increased their rates in three years, some in as many as five years. The cost of living has increased every year and photographers have been forced to lower their standard of living just to stay in business.

At the same time the cost of digital cameras has dropped substantially whilst their quality has improved, lowering the barriers to entry into the industry. Improvements in software have made it easier to fix mistakes resulting in clients being able to work with photographers of lower skill levels. Every year the photography universities, colleges and schools churn out more graduates, most of whom will never be able to enter the industry as working photographers. I have never seen the industry more competitive than it is right now.

The challenge with this is that it is a 'buyers market'. Clients are spoilt for choice, are economically dominant (they have the money that we need to survive) and tend to dictate the rates and terms on a take it or leave it basis. Many photographers take it, without doing their costings properly, and end up leaving the industry bankrupt, jaded and bitter.

Photography is a business and businesses exist to make profit. Your photography business needs to be financially viable to thrive. It's not good enough to survive. Survival is for tough times, seasons that pass. Your business needs to thrive so that you can draw the salary you deserve as your reward for the time you put in, and make a profit as your reward for the risk you take being self-employed.

RETURN ON INVESTMENT (ROI)

Making a return on your investment sounds obvious, but are you aware of the investment you have made in yourself as a photographer?

Today it costs approximately R35 000 per year to study photography at a government subsidised tertiary institution and between R50 000 - R60 000 per year at a private institution, for fees only. Books, materials, stationary and other costs must still be added. Most accredited photography qualifications require three to four years of study resulting in a total investment of approximately R200 000.

On top of this starting out as a photographer requires capital investment. You need equipment to work with, a car to get around in, a computer to work on, a mobile phone as well as other items just to get going, resulting in another investment of approximately R200 000 depending on what you start with.

So by now you've invested R400 000 into your fledgling career as a photographer just to get to the point of being able to take on commissions.

If you invest R400 000 into an investment account with modest returns you are likely to make a guaranteed return of 10% per year. There are more risky investments with higher returns but for the sake of argument we'll work with 10%.

Over a period of ten years your R400 000 investment will grow into **R 1 082 816,60** with compound interest, calculated monthly, at an interest rate of 10% per year, without you doing anything further.

The question is, will you be able to grow your investment in yourself as a photographer to produce better returns in ten years? If not, is it really sensible to do it? You're better off investing your money and doing something else.

However, if your desire to be a professional photographer burns so deeply in your soul that it cannot be ignored, then there is a way. Patience, passion, tenacity, perseverance, sheer determination, insight and a level head.

DEFINING YOUR CLIENTS

The photography market is extremely broad. Basically, anything that you are interested in can be, and is photographed. From people to places to objects the demand for photographic images is high. Imagine the world we live without photographs at all. Photography is a form of visual communication and is just as, if not more effective than written communication.

Emerging photographers tend to be enthusiastic and hungry for work, wanting to prove themselves and break into an already over traded market. As a result of this they are easily and frequently exploited. Just because a potential client approaches you to shoot for them does not mean you have to accept the assignment. It should always be worth your while, if not then it's advisable to turn it down. A good, worthwhile client is someone who:.

- ☑ Recognises and acknowledges the financial value of your creativity.
- ☑ Is open, honest and transparent about the full scope of work of the job.
- ☑ Pays you what you are worth.
- ☑ Pays their invoices in full within the agreed time period.
- ☑ Honours the agreements (especially license and payment agreements) they enter into with you.

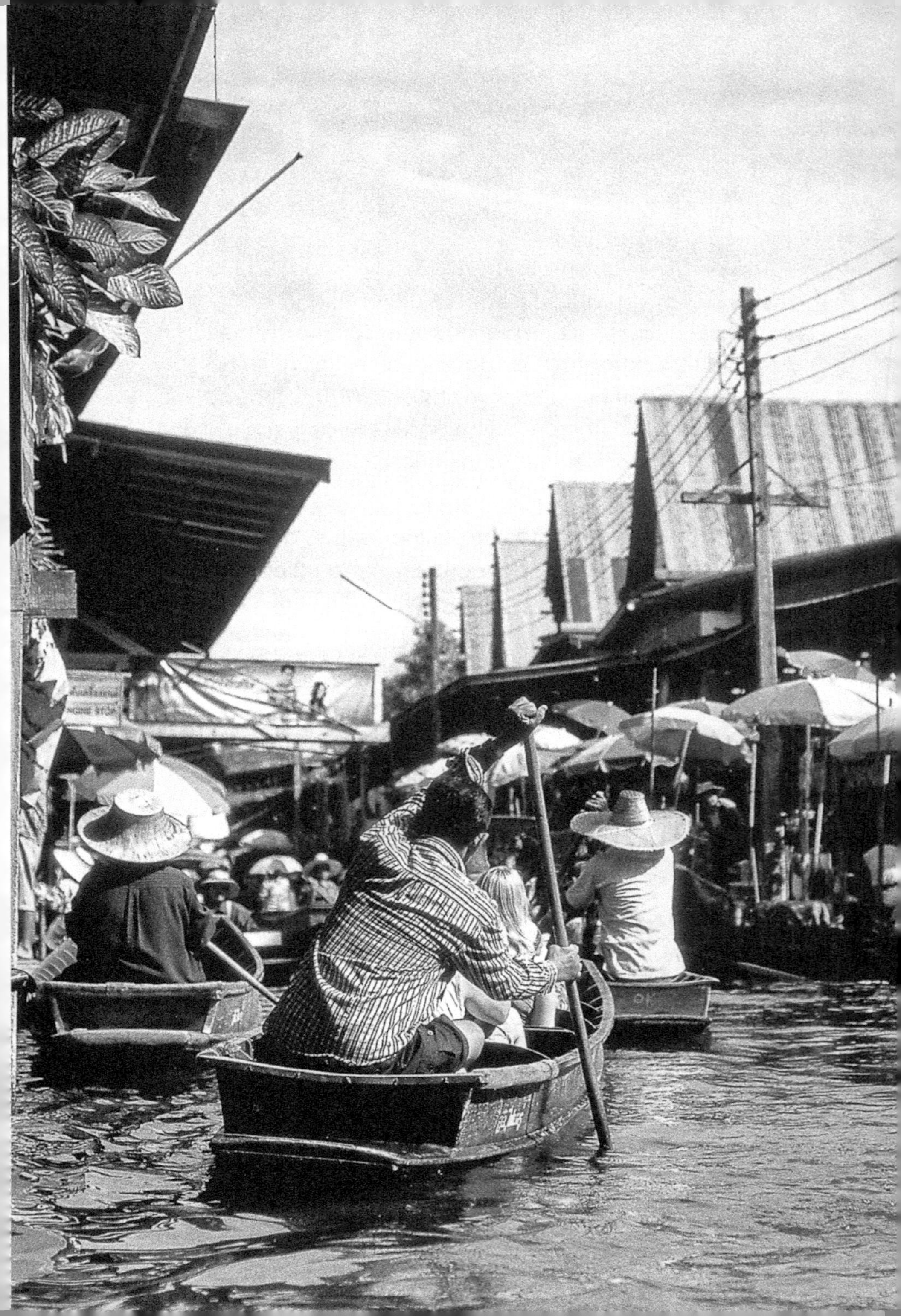

CHAPTER 2

MARKETS

"Photography is not about the thing photographed. It is about how that thing looks photographed."

Garry Winogrand

There are a number of markets for professional photography. Photographers are paid according to the market their images are used in NOT for what they shoot (the subject). The same photograph of the same subject will command different fees in different markets.

The main markets for photography are:

1. ADVERTISING PHOTOGRAPHY

The primary purpose of advertising photography is to produce an image that draws attention to a product, service, or event in a public medium to promote sales or attendance *e.g. a billboard advertising beer*. The image serves a twofold purpose. The first to draw attention to the concept, the second to convey information about the concept. These images are generally created with an advertising agency, design firm or with a corporate in-house marketing team. Advertising BUR (Base Usage Rates) tend to be the highest BUR in commercial photography due to the high level of creative input required from the photographer (intellectual property) as well as the fact that the photographer receives no visible credit for the image in it's final use (no byline).

An advertising assignment begins with a brief from the advertising agency, usually compiled by the Art Director or Creative Director of the advertising campaign. The brief should be received in writing and should clearly convey the use, subject, action, location and required result. The photographer costs and executes the shoot according to this brief which is why it is essential for the brief to be clear, accurate and in writing.

2. CORPORATE / DESIGN PHOTOGRAPHY

This category is photographs created for use by businesses in their corporate material such as annual reports, presentations and staff training. This does not extend to advertising use.

The use of the image is what defines it's corporate nature, not the subject.

Corporate photography is used to illustrate company information/literature, for example an annual report. Annual reports for large businesses tend to be well designed and illustrated and use a number of images from portraits of the directors and staff members to pictures illustrating what the business does.

Companies tend to either outsource the design, including photography, to design agencies or have their own in-house design team. This is why this category is know as Corporate/Design as the photographer may be commissioned either by a company or design agency.

Internal communications letters or magazines are also classified as corporate photography. i.e. magazines that are not sold by the company but are used within the company to communicate with their customers and staff.

The Corporate/Design BUR should be a photographers full, normal BUR and does not include a by-line, unless asserted by the photographer. BURs are explained in more detail in a later chapter.

Photography used to promote a product or service other than within a corporate structure is classified as

Advertising Photography, such as print media ads, point of sale, catalogues, billboards, ambient displays, etc.

3. SOCIAL PHOTOGRAPHY

Social photography is photographs taken at social events of the people attending the event and activities taking place at the event such as cocktail parties, weddings and other social events. Social photography tends to be one of the greatest employers of photographers as many social events occur frequently and the organisers of the events require the event to be photographically documented.

Social photography is either commissioned through a company, especially Public Relations (PR) companies, or by private individuals (private commissions) hosting a birthday party, wedding or other life event.

Social photography provides one of the easiest points of entry into professional photography as the equipment and skill level requirements are quite low. It tends to be 'point and shoot' photography with a camera and flash and does not require high end, advanced equipment. Like Corporate/Design Photography Social Photography should be a photographers full, normal BUR.

4. ADVERTORIALS / PROMOTIONS

An Advertorial (or promotion) is strictly speaking advertising. The difference is that the publication's editorial team designs the advertorial instead of an external advertising or marketing agency. Advertorials are often more copy (words) intensive and are intended to be read by the reader as an 'article' of interest, created to illustrate and usually sell a product or service in a magazine. Advertorials often look similar to print media adverts but the base usage rate paid for advertorials is less than half of an advertising BUR.

Advertorials are an invention of the publishing industry. Print media adverts tend to be expensive for the advertiser as the advertiser needs to pay an advertising agency to conceptualise and design the advert and then pay the magazine to place the advert in the magazine. The publishers of magazines realised that by designing the advert for the client using their editorial staff they could incentivise advertisers who would normally have been deterred by the cost to advertise in their magazine.

Unfortunately they managed to convince photographers at the time to settle for a reduced 'Advertorial BUR' in return for a byline (photo credit). It is a photographers legal moral right to be named as the author of their work, if asserted, so essentially the publishers managed to reduce photographers fees in exchange for a credit that was already a photographers legal right. This is one of the many reasons why it is so important for photographers to know their rights.

5. EDITORIAL PHOTOGRAPHY

Editorial photography is photographs made to illustrate a story or idea within the context of a magazine, newspaper or news web site. These are usually assigned by the magazine and are essentially documentary photography assignments, although fashion, beauty, food and decor are included.

Editorial photography is the use of photographs in an editorial context, i.e. specifically NOT FOR ADVERTISING of any nature including promotions, to illustrate or accompany a written article. The photograph may be used on it's own with a caption not accompanying an article to convey a powerful message, as a pictorial.

The use of the image is what defines it's editorial nature, not the subject.

The image must be accompanied by a 'by-line' or credit near the photograph that clearly displays the photographer's name. This by-line is deemed to have a financial value as it serves as advertising for the photographer which is why editorial rates are the lowest of the Base Usage Rates (BUR). Strictly speaking, should a publication fail to include the photographer's by-line it should then pay the photographer the full commercial BUR for the use of the image.

The most prestigious place for a photographer's work to be featured in an editorial context is on the cover of the publication. Cover photographs also command the highest fee for non-commissioned photographs.

6. FINE ART PHOTOGRAPHY

Photographs created to fulfil an artistic, creative vision, to be sold directly to the customer as a work of art, usually through an art gallery or art auction, are classified as fine art photography. The subject of a photograph does not determine it's status as fine art but rather its use.

The artistic quality and integrity of a photograph is highly subjective. Since most fine art photography is bought for decorative purposes its value is perceived by the purchaser based on the status of the photographer and the aesthetic quality of the image to the buyer. The works of serious fine art photographers are extremely valuable. To date, Andreas Gursky's "*Rhein II*" holds the world record for the highest price paid for a photographic fine art print. In 2011, a print was auctioned for £2.7 million ($4.3 million at the time).

7. PHOTO LIBRARY / STOCK IMAGES

Photographs created by the photographer sold on the photographer's behalf by an image library (photo library) fall within this category. The photographs may be used in any market from Advertising to Corporate and Editorial on a royalty free (RF) and rights managed (RM) basis, determined by the photo library.

Royalty Free (RF) stock photography, also known as micro stock, is largely responsible for the degradation of the photographic industry and perceived value of photography. The buyer of a RF image may use the image for any purpose, in any media, without paying royalties for the use. RF images tend to be cheap as the success of the RF business model is derived from volume sales. The result of this is that clients have become accustomed to paying very little for the unrestricted use of photographs, creating the expectation that this applies to all photography.

Rights Managed (RM) stock photography is far healthier for the photographic industry as the rights to use each image are negotiated by the photo library with the buyer and the price determined according to the use. The use of the image for advertising purpose commands a fee a lot higher than editorial use. Buyouts apply to RM images radically increasing the fee and therefore financial return for the photographer.

8. PRIVATE COMMISSIONS

Private commissions are photographs created directly for the end user of the images such as portraits or family events like weddings or events of religious family significance such as bar-mitzvahs. In the USA private commissions are referred to as 'Retail Photography'.

Family portraiture is big business that is unfortunately dominated by 'semi-professional' photographers, many of whom are not financially dependent on the income they receive from their photography as they have a supportive spouse or partner. The barriers to entry are extremely low as an entry level camera and level of skill have become the acceptable standard. Many 'family photographers' rates are so low that they are actually paying their clients to work for them without even realising it, that is, they are not covering their true costs.

It is important to know and be able to distinguish between these different markets as the rates that photographers are paid differ between these markets. Photographers are not paid according to the subject that they shoot but rather according to which market the photographs are used in/for.

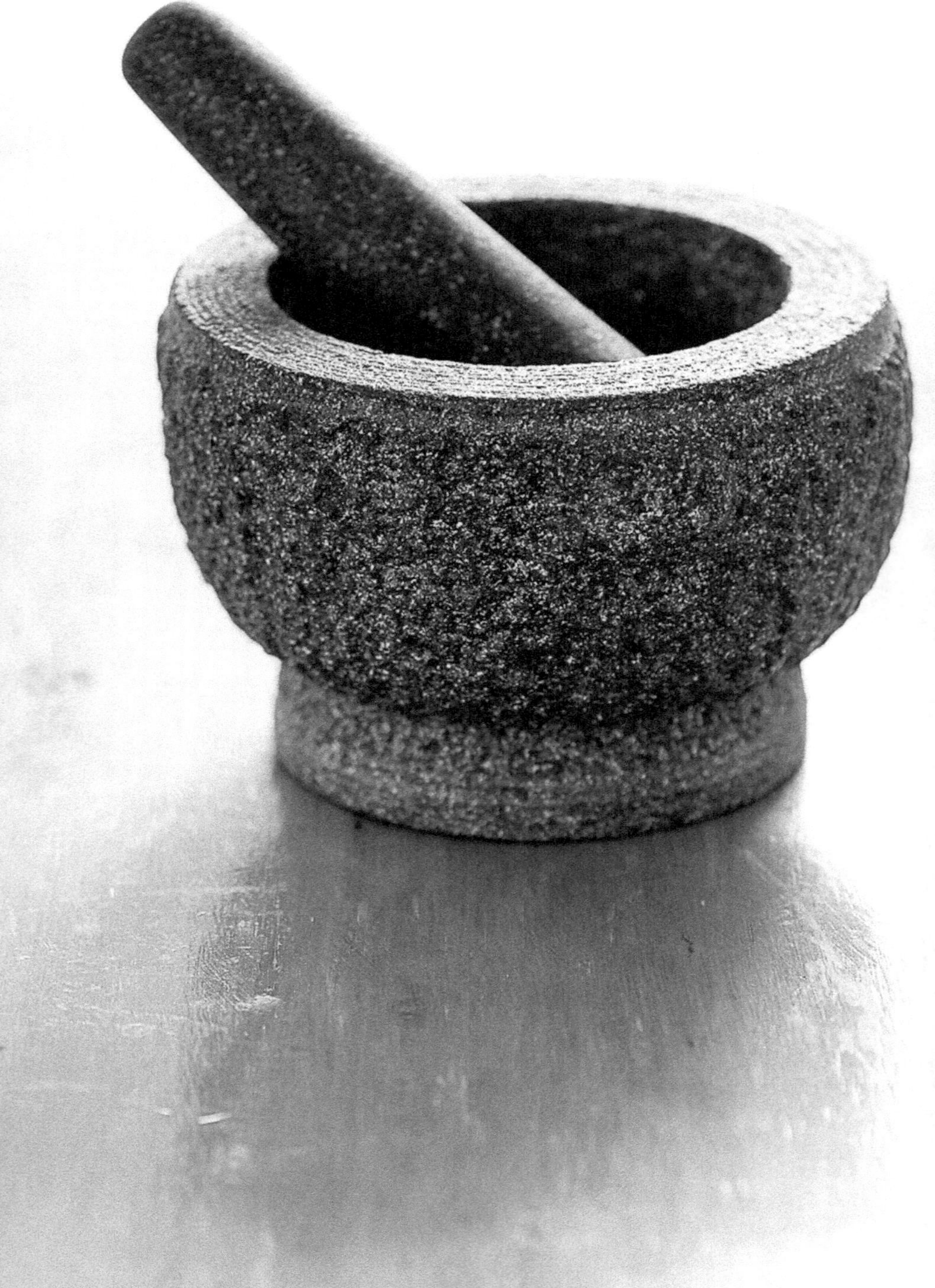

CHAPTER 3

INTELLECTUAL PROPERTY

"To deny people their Human Rights is to challenge their very humanity."

Nelson Mandela

WHAT IS INTELLECTUAL PROPERTY?

Intellectual Property (IP) is a legal term describing the fact that people have rights to their creativity and innovation. IP rights cannot be held over ideas, only over the way ideas are expressed in material form such as designs, inventions, film, music, painting, photography, sculpture and writing.

Protecting your IP rights in something you create enables you to sell the license for use thereof, or to claim financial settlement when others use your work(s) for financial gain.

According to the World Intellectual Property Organisation (WIPO):

Intellectual property (IP) refers to creations of the mind: inventions, literary and artistic works, and symbols, names, images, and designs used in commerce.

IP is divided into two categories:

Industrial property, which includes inventions (patents), trademarks, industrial designs, and geographic indications of source;

Copyright, which includes literary and artistic works such as novels, poems and plays, films, musical works, artistic works such as drawings, paintings, photographs and sculptures, and architectural designs.

Rights related to copyright include those of performing artists in their performances, producers of phonograms in their recordings, and those of broadcasters in their radio and television programs. [1]

The World Intellectual Property Organisation (WIPO) is an international organisation dedicated to promoting creativity and innovation by ensuring that the rights of creators and owners of intellectual property are protected worldwide, and that inventors and authors are thus recognised and rewarded for their ingenuity. [2]

WIPO is a specialised agency of the United Nations, established as a forum for its Member States to create and harmonise rules and practices to protect intellectual property rights.

The United Nations values the protection of intellectual property so highly that it enshrined it in the Universal Declaration of Human Rights.

Article 27

Everyone has the right to freely participate in the cultural life of the community, to enjoy the arts and to share in scientific advancement and its benefits.

Everyone has the right to the protection of the moral and material interests resulting from any scientific, literary or artistic production of which he is the author.

Both the Berne Convention and the United Nations Universal Declaration of Human Rights specify that the Author of the works has the right to protection NOT the

---

[1] http://www.wipo.int/about-ip/en/

[2] http://www.wipo.int/copyright/en/

owner of the copyright therein, if the owner of the copyright is not the Author of the works.

The Republic of South Africa is a member of the United Nations and a signatory to the WIPO.

According to WIPO, "*Copyright and related rights protect the rights of authors, performers, producers and broadcasters, and contribute to the cultural and economic development of nations. This protection fulfils a decisive role in clarifying the rights of different stakeholders and the relationship between them and the public.*

The purpose of copyright and related rights is to encourage a dynamic creative culture, while returning value to creators so that they can lead a dignified economic existence, and to provide widespread, affordable access to content for the public."

Copyright protects the right of the Author (creator) to reproduce the work in any manner or form unless otherwise agreed. Limited private or personal use of the work by others is allowed without payment. The ownership of copyright ensures that the creator of the work can earn an income from the commercial use of a significant part of the work, or through unacknowledged use of the work.

In many countries copyright can be assigned, sold or licensed to others. Some countries do not allow the separation of authorship and ownership of copyright. The Author is the owner of the copyright to the works by default and cannot assign the copyright but they can sell license for use of the works.

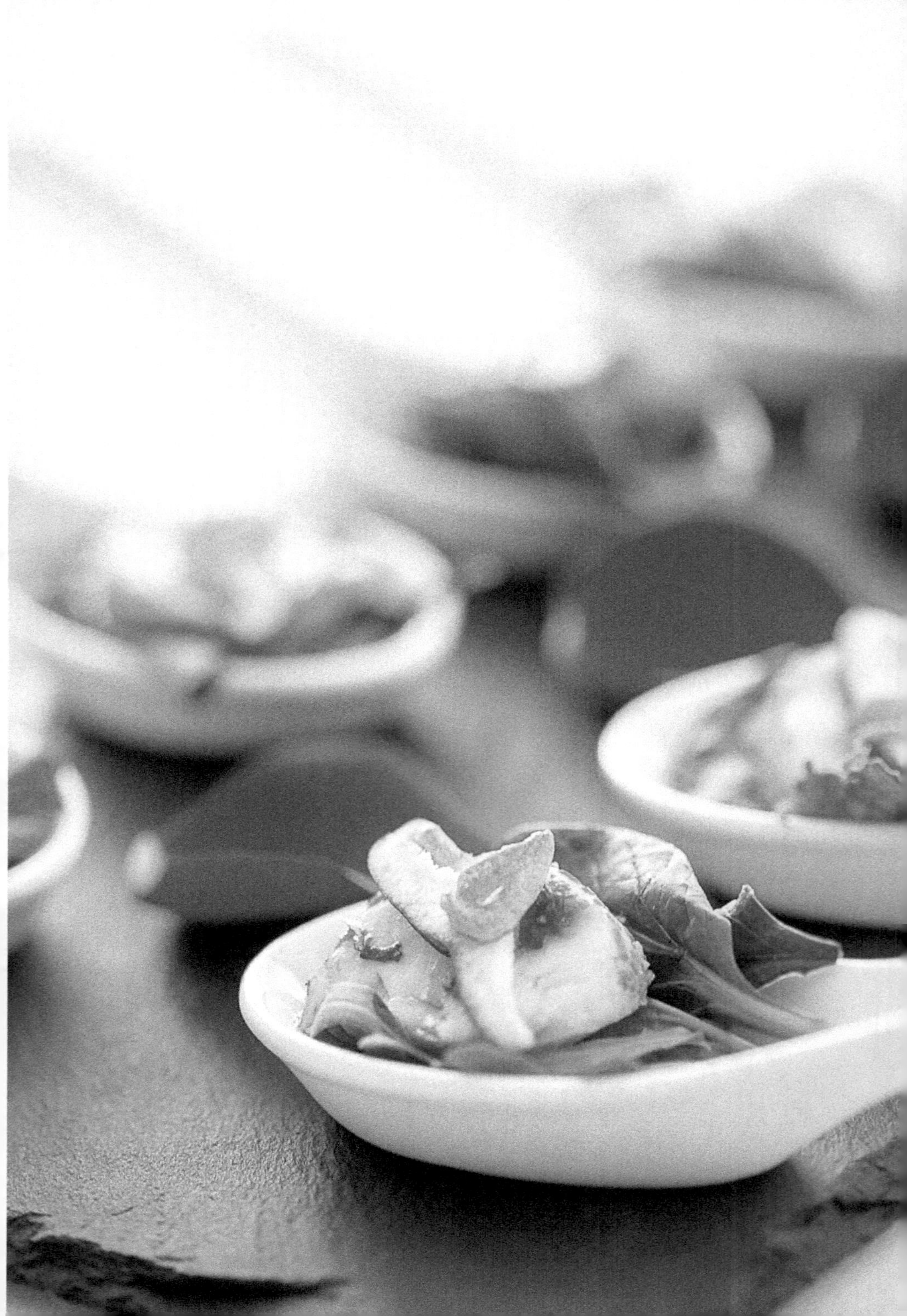

CHAPTER 4

COPYRIGHT

FOR PHOTOGRAPHERS IN SOUTH AFRICA

"If we don't have the key, we can't open whatever we don't have that it unlocks. So what purpose would be served in finding whatever need be unlocked, which we don't have, without first having found the key what unlocks it?"

Captain Jack Sparrow

Photographers copyright is currently a highly contentious issue with the explosion of the internet and the blatant theft of images from photographers web sites, or perhaps worse, the claiming of license to use and sub-license images by social media web sites and networks like Facebook and Instagram. However, it is not all doom and gloom.

It is essential for photographers to know the truth about copyright, especially in South Africa, as the true financial value in photography is not in day rates or selling a picture but is in owning the copyright to your photographs empowering you to sell the license for use of your work.

Bill Gates is one of the wealthiest men in the world today. He did not make his fortune selling software, he made it selling license for use of his software. He understood the true value of intellectual property, as does the government and businesses that exploit photographers in South Africa. Even though many businesses intimidate photographers with contracts to sign on a 'take it or leave it' basis, claiming ownership of the IP to their work, every contract is negotiable. The successful negotiation of a contract starts with knowing the truth about your rights.

Copyright is a legislated right that forms part of Intellectual Property (IP) law. Other IP rights are patents, trade marks and registered designs. Unlike other IP rights, copyright is an automatic right and does not have to be registered to be enforced. The name copyright is actually the right to prevent copying and in Europe is also referred to as 'author's right' or 'originators right'.

The copyright law of the Republic of South Africa (RSA) that is applicable to photographers is very different from that of most first world countries. The international standard for copyright for photographers is that the photographer owns the copyright to all images created by the photographer, regardless of who commissions the images and what the images will be used for, unless an agreement is entered into specifying otherwise.

The basic underlying principle of the protection of copyright is that the work must be original. This means that the work must originate from the author (creator) and must not be copied from another authors work. The work should be the result of the author's independent labour and not an imitation of an earlier work. There is a fine line between copying, appropriating and referencing.

Copying is the act of making something similar or identical to an original. The problem is telling which is the original and which is the copy. The best example of this in photography is a photographer photographing another photographers photograph, the challenge being in determining which is the original.

Appropriating is a nice way of saying stealing and is to take something for someone's own use without the owner's permission. Millions of photographs are appropriated from the internet every day, mostly illegal blatant copyright infringement.

Referencing is legal and is the act of mentioning or alluding to someone else's work, using their work as a source of information or inspiration and then creating a new, original work.

South Africa's Copyright Act of 1978 (Act 98 of 1978, as amended) covers literary, musical and artistic works, cinematograph films, sound recordings, broadcasts, program carrying signals, published editions and computer programs. 'Artistic work' includes paintings, sculptures, drawings, engravings and photographs, *irrespective of the artistic quality thereof.*

MORAL RIGHTS

Moral rights are quite simply the right of the Author (Photographer) to be named as the Author of the work he/she creates as well as to object to the distortion or mutilation of that work.

Section 20 of the Copyright Act refers to Moral Rights.

(1) Notwithstanding the transfer of the copyright in a literary, musical or artistic work, in a cinematograph film or in a computer program, the author shall have the right to claim authorship of the work, and to object to any distortion, mutilation or other modification of the work where such action is or would be prejudicial to the honour or reputation of the author.

(2) Any infringement of the provisions of this section shall be treated as an infringement of copyright under Chapter 2, and for the purposes of the provisions of the said Chapter the author shall be deemed to be the owner of the copyright in question. [S. 20 substituted by s. 19 of Act No. 125 of 1992.]

The Author of the work must assert the right to be named as the author of that work and again, this should form part of your basic business documentation.

In advertising photography it is common for the author of the work to be required to waive the right to be named, one of the reasons why advertising photography rates are higher than the other markets rates. The advertising agency is credited as the author of the advert in magazine adverts.

OWNERSHIP OF COPYRIGHT

The part of the South Africa copyright act that is particularly relevant to photography is section 21(1) under the heading *'Ownership of copyright'*.

a) *Subject to the provisions of this section, the ownership of any copyright conferred by section 3 or 4 on any work shall vest in the author or, in the case of a work of joint authorship, in the co-authors of the work.*

Section 21(1)a) of the Copyright Act clearly states that photographers who create their own images (not commissioned) own the copyright to those images by default and are entitled to sell the License for Use of the images. This is in line with internationally accepted copyright for photographers standards. However, sections (b)-(d) are the sections that are problematic for photographers in South Africa.

b) *Where a literary or artistic work is made by an author in the course of his employment by the proprietor of a newspaper, magazine or similar periodical under a contract of service or apprenticeship, and is so made for the purpose of publication in a newspaper, magazine or similar periodical, the said proprietor shall be the owner of the copyright in the work in so far as the copyright relates to publication of the work in any newspaper, magazine or similar periodical or to reproduction of the work for the purpose of its being so published, but in all other respects the author shall be the owner of any copyright subsisting in the work by virtue of section 3 or 4.*

Section 21(1)b) states that if a photographer is employed by a periodical (newspaper/magazine) then the employer owns the copyright to the images the photographer creates during their employment by default. Unless otherwise agreed. This only applies to photographs that are created by the photographer during work hours. Any images created by the photographer outside of work hours are not covered by this.

c) Where a person commissions the taking of a photograph, the painting or drawing of a portrait, the making of a gravure, the making of a cinematograph film or the making of a sound recording and pays or agrees to pay for it in money or money's worth, and the work is made in pursuance of that commission, such person shall, subject to the provisions of paragraph (b), be the owner of any copyright subsisting therein by virtue of section 3 or 4.

Section 21(1)c) states that should a photographer be commissioned to create photographs and the photographs are created in pursuance of that commission, then the commissioning agent owns the copyright to the commissioned images by default. Unless otherwise agreed.

> *d) Where in a case not falling within either paragraph (b) or (c) a work is made in the course of the author's employment by another person under a contract of service or apprenticeship, that other person shall be the owner of any copyright subsisting in the work by virtue of section 3 or 4.*

Section 21(1)d) states that should a photographer be employed in any other capacity then the employer will own the copyright to images created by the photographer during his/her employment. Unless otherwise agreed.

Section 21(1)e) is the section that empowers photographers to agree otherwise.

> *e) Paragraphs (b), (c) and (d) shall in any particular case have effect subject to any agreement excluding the operation thereof and subject to the provisions of section 20.*

This means that whilst the employer/commissioning agent owns the copyright by default in Sections 21(1)b)-d), the Author (photographer) is empowered to change this by mutual agreement. This can form part of the Photographers job documentation for ease of use.

Section 21(2) states that:

Ownership of any copyright conferred by section 5 shall initially vest in the state or the international organisation concerned, and not the author.

Section 5(2) states that:

Copyright shall be conferred by this section on every work which is illegible for copyright and which is made by or under the direction or control of the state or such international organisations as may be prescribed.

Essentially this means that the copyright to photographs created by employees of, or commissioned by the state, is the property of the state, or prescribed international organisations, for the lifespan of the copyright.

The Copyright Act is applicable to the Republic of South Africa ONLY and does not extend beyond it's borders. Images commissioned in South Africa for use in South Africa that are then used outside of South Africa fall under the World Trade Organisation Agreement on Trade Related Aspects of Intellectual Property Rights (TRIPs), that includes the Berne Convention.

South Africa has been a World Trade Organisation (WTO) member since 1 January 1995 including the World Trade Organisation Agreement on Trade Related Aspects of Intellectual Property Rights (TRIPs) that includes the Berne Convention for the Protection of Literary and Artistic Works. South Africa has been a member of the Berne Convention since 1928. The USA became a member of the Berne Convention in 1989. Prior to this a bilateral agreement existed between the RSA and the USA that was withdrawn in 1991.

The TRIPS Agreement was established to protect intellectual property rights internationally including photography. In terms of this agreement the copyright legislation of the country in which the images are used applies. That is, if a photographer is commissioned to create images in South Africa and the images are then used in Germany then German copyright law applies. In this case the commissioning agent would have to buy the rights to use the image in Germany from the photographer.

The Berne Convention for the protection of Literary and Artistic works was established in 1886. Countries that are signatories to the Berne Convention, like South Africa, are bound to protect the rights of authors from other member countries in the same way as they protect their own. This is known as the principle of national treatment. The copyright is by default the automatic property of the author of the work who may assign the copyright or sell license for use thereof, in most member countries, regardless of whether the author owns the copyright to their work in their own country.

Article 9(1) of the Berne Convention states:

"Authors of literary and artistic works protected by this convention shall have the exclusive right of authorising the reproduction of these works, in any manner or form".

Article 9(2) states:

"It shall be a matter for legislation in the countries of the union to permit the reproduction of such works in certain special cases, provided that such reproduction does not conflict with a normal exploitation of the work

and does not unreasonably prejudice the legitimate interests of the author."

According to Part 2, Section 1 of TRIPs, *"Members shall comply with Articles 1 through 21 of the Berne Convention and the appendix thereto"*. There is no special provision in these treaties that determines any rights for an 'owner' of copyright as opposed to an 'author' of that work. The rights are very clearly the Author's.

Despite local copyright law, the international position is that the author is protected by the copyright laws of the signatory countries and any use of a photograph outside South Africa by the local owner, who is not the author of the work, amounts to copyright infringement.

The current South African Copyright Act very clearly discriminates against photographers in favour of their employer/commissioning agent. Whilst internationally it is a photographers right to *"lead a dignified economic existence"* from the sale of the license to use their work this is currently not the case in South Africa.

Perhaps the most well known example of this is the iconic photograph of fatally wounded twelve year old Hector Pieterson being carried by Mbuyisa Makhubo, with Hector's seventeen year old sister Antoinette Pieterson right beside them, on 16th June 1976 captured by Sam Nzima. The iconic photograph, that helped to bring about the end of apartheid, was published by *The World* newspaper, who sold the image throughout the world benefitting handsomely from it's sale, with none of the royalties paid to Sam Nzima. Sam Nzima continued to struggle to earn a dignified economic existence. After years of fighting for the rights to his photograph Mr. Nzima was finally rewarded in 1998 when the copyright to his image was finally assigned to him, after The Independent Newspaper Group bought The Argus Group. Mr. Nzima now sells the license for use thereof using some of the proceeds to fund upcoming photojournalists studies.

Please remember that whilst the current copyright law in South Africa discriminates against photographers who are employed or commissioned, according to *Section 21(1)a)* the ownership of copyright vests in the author (photographer) by default if the photographer has not been commissioned or does not create the image(s) during his/her employment.

Furthermore the assignment (transferring of ownership) of copyright must be done in writing and signed by the owner of the copyright being assigned.

Section 21(1)e) empowers photographers to override Sections *21(1)b) - d)* by mutual agreement.

COPYRIGHT PROTECTION

Copyright protection by law is automatic for eligible works.

A photograph is defined as an 'artistic work' in *Section 1(1)(iii)*, *"irrespective of the artistic quality thereof"*.

Works created by a *"qualified person"* do not have to be registered to be protected in South Africa. A qualified person is defined in *Section 3(1) as:*

(a) *in the case of an individual, a person who is a South Africa citizen or who is domiciled or resident in the Republic of South Africa.*

(b) *in the case of a juristic person, a body incorporated under the laws of the Republic of South Africa.*

Except for cinematograph films, which are possible to register in South Africa, the most common ways to protect copyrighted works against infringements would be to mark works with copyright notices and to enter into written copyright and/or license for use agreements.

Copyright notices serve as a warning to third parties that copyright subsists in a work. Generally, copyright notices should include the following elements:

- *The international copyright symbol i.e. ©*
- *The name of the owner*
- *The year in which the work was created*
- *Example: © John Doe 2012*

In South Africa, the Dramatic, Artistic, Literary Rights Organisation (DALRO) is the only collective rights organisation which receive mandates from authors and publishers to license the use of their dramatic, artistic and literary works. DALRO administers the license schemes for dramatic, artistic and literary works, collects and pays over royalties to authors and publishers. DALRO is a nonprofit organisation and requires an administrative fee for this service.

It should however be noted that legal copyright protection is automatic and works do not need to be registered with DALRO to be protected by the Copyright Act.

ASSIGNING AND LICENSING

The owner of the copyright has the default exclusive legal right to do, or authorise the doing of the following, according to *Section 7:*

- Reproduce the work in any manner or form
- Publish the work if it is unpublished
- Include the work in a cinematograph film or television broadcast, performing the work in public
- Cause a television or other programme, which includes the work to be transmitted in a diffusion service, unless the service transmits a lawful broadcast including the work, and is operated by the original broadcaster
- Make an adaption of the work

This means that the work may not be reproduced without the Author's permission in any manner or form.

An adaption of the work is defined in *Section 1(1)(c)* as *"an artistic work, includes transformation of the work in such a manner that the original or substantial features thereof remain recognisable"*.

According to *Section 22* copyright is:

- *"...movable property by assignment, testamentary disposition or operation of law"*. In other words the ownership of copyright can be transferred (assigned), bought and sold or inherited.

- The assignment of copyright, or the exclusive license to use, must be *"in writing and signed by or on behalf of the assignor, the licensor or, in the case of exclusive sublicense, the exclusive sub-licenser, as the case may be"*.
- A non-exclusive license to use *"may be written or oral, or may be inferred from conduct, and may be revoked at any time ... except as the contract may provide, or by further contract."*
- An assignment, license or testamentary disposition may be granted in respect of future works, in other works that are still to be created.
- A license granted in respect of copyright is binding on every successor unless mutually otherwise agreed.

The above means that the owner of the copyright to a work is empowered to sell the license for use of the work and subsequent owners must honour the license, unless otherwise mutually agreed in writing and signed. Copyright can be inherited as part of a deceased estate, an important point for photographers to remember.

COPYRIGHT INFRINGEMENT

The infringement of copyright to photographs is an offence in South Africa. The Copyright Act 98 of 1978 (as amended) section 27, under the heading *Penalties and proceedings in respect of dealings which infringe copyright*, says:

(1) Any person who at a time when copyright subsists in a work, without the authority of the owner of the copyright

- *(a)* *makes for sale or hire;*
- *(b)* *sells or lets for hire or by way of trade offers or exposes for sale or hire;*
- *(c)* *by way of trade exhibits in public;*
- *(d)* *imports into the Republic otherwise than for his private or domestic use;*
- *(e)* *distributes for purposes of trade; or*
- *(f)* *distributes for any other purposes to such an extent that the owner of the copyright is prejudicially affected, articles which he knows to be infringing copies of the work, shall be guilty of an offence.[Sub-s. (1) substituted by s. 11 (a) of Act No. 52 of 1984 and by s 3. of Act No. 61 of 1989.]*

Paragraph 6 goes on to say:

(6) A person convicted of an offence under this section shall be liable—

- *(a)* *in the case of a first conviction, to a fine not exceeding five thousand rand or to imprisonment for a period not exceeding three years or to both such fine and such imprisonment, for each article to which the offence relates;*
- *(b)* *in any other case, to a fine not exceeding ten thousand rand or to imprisonment for a period*

> *not exceeding five years or to both such fine and such imprisonment, for each article to which the offence relates.[Sub-s. (6) substituted by s. 11 (b) of Act No. 52 of 1984 and by s. 24 (a) of Act No. 125 of 1992.]*

Copyright is infringed when someone does something with the copyrighted work(s) that the owner of the copyright has the exclusive right to do, without the owner's consent. Infringement occurs if either the whole or a substantial part of the work is misused. Contrary to the way it appears a substantial part refers to the quality and not the quantity of the work that is used.

Should an exclusive license for use exist for a work that is infringed then the licensee and/or sublicensee has the same rights of action and is entitled to the same remedies as the owner of the copyright, in terms of the rights allocated in the license.

Section 24 stipulates the action the owner/exclusive license for use holder of copyright can take in the case of infringement, saying that "*infringements of copyright shall be actionable at the suit of the owner of the copyright*" empowering the owner to claim "*damages, interdict, delivery of infringing copies*". The burden of proof however rests with the owner/exclusive license for use holder, to the degree that *Section 24 (2)* says, "*Where in an action for infringement of copyright it is proved or admitted that an infringement was committed but that at the time of the infringement the defendant was not aware and had no reasonable grounds for suspecting that copyright subsisted in the work to which the action relates, the plaintiff shall not be entitled under this section to any damages against the defendant in respect of the infringement."*

This is clearly a startling point as the onus is on you to prove that the infringer knowingly and willingly infringed your copyright, which if you can't, you will not receive damages for their illegal use of your image(s). The most common place that copyright infringement of images occurs is the internet, from photographers web sites. You can overcome this by displaying a clearly visible notice on your web site like:

"The contents of this web site are protected by international copyright, all rights reserved."

An even more effective way of ensuring that an offender cannot claim they did not know is by placing a copyright notice on every image you upload as a watermark in the form of:

© [Copyright Owner's Name] [Copyright Year]

For example: © Deryck van Steenderen, 2016

Please remember that the name of the owner of the copyright must be displayed, so if you created the image and are not the owner of the copyright therein, then the owner's name must be displayed.

Section 27 states that any person who knowingly and willingly infringes copyright shall be guilty of a criminal offence and may be fined and/or imprisoned depending on the nature and extent of the infringement.

RESOLVING COPYRIGHT INFRINGEMENT

The simplest and most cost efficient way of resolving copyright infringement is to invoice the offender for the use of the work(s), at the applicable standard industry rates, with a covering letter informing them of their infringement and the reason for the invoice. You can include a 'cease and desist' or 'take down' notice in the letter as well, instructing them to remove your image(s) and not to use it anymore, referring to *Section 27* with the option of criminal charges being pressed as an alternative. The option of handing the invoice over for debt collection is a far more financially efficient solution than suing in a civil court for breach of copyright, should the offender refuse to pay.

Copyright infringement is an unfortunate side effect of the internet. Many internet users seem to think that they can use images found on the internet for anything they please as the images are in the 'public domain'. This is incorrect. Images on the internet are protected by the same copyright laws as images published in other media. An image does not have to be watermarked in order to be protected by copyright on the internet just as an image does not have to be watermarked to be protected by copyright in a magazine. It is however good practice to include a copyright notice on a website in order to prove that a person knowingly and willingly infringed your copyright by taking an image from your website.

There are a number of online resources that provide reverse image search functionality to determine the number of websites that are using an image, such as [3]Tin Eye and Google's Reverse Image Search using internet browsers like Chrome 5+, Safari 5+, Internet Explorer 9+ and Firefox 4+. Both work on the basis of uploading an image and running a search. The websites using the same image come up showing the pages on which the image(s) are being used. You can then determine whether the website has bought the rights to use the image(s) from you or not and take action accordingly.

GENERAL EXCEPTIONS FROM COPYRIGHT PROTECTION

Certain acts are allowed under the copyright act, without the copyright owner of the artistic works permission. The copyright in an artistic work (photograph) is not infringed if it is reproduced or included in a cinematograph film or television broadcast, or transmission or diffusion service, if the work is included in the background, or incidental to the principal matters represented in the film, broadcast or transmission, or if the work is permanently situated in a street, square or public place, according to *Section 15(1)-(3)*.

FAIR USE/FAIR DEALING/FAIR PRACTICE

Fair Use is the American term for Fair Dealing, the term used by ex Commonwealth countries and the United Kingdom.

[3] www.tineye.com

In South Africa, fair dealing is listed in the Copyright Act of 1978 (Act 98 of 1978 as amended). Fair dealing is described in section 12(1) of the Act, sections 13 to 19 explain various exceptions to copyright. The author's moral rights (Section 20), may also have an impact on a fair dealing ruling if infringed.

According to this Act,

Copyright shall not be infringed by any fair dealing with a literary or musical work

- *(a) for the purposes of research or private study by, or the personal or private use of, the person using the work;*
- *(b) for the purposes of criticism or review of that work or of another work; or*
- *(c) for the purpose of reporting current events*
  - *(i) in a newspaper, magazine or similar periodical; or*
  - *(ii) by means of broadcasting or in a cinematograph film;*

Provided that, in the case of paragraphs (b) and (c)(i), the source shall be mentioned, as well as the name of the author if it appears on the work.

COPYRIGHT LIFESPAN

Copyright has a lifespan. The lifespan of copyright differs from country to country. It also differs for various forms of creativity.

In South Africa the lifespan of copyright to photographs expires 50 years after the work is made available to the public (published). If the photograph is not published within 50 years of its making, copyright expires 50 years after the photograph is made. It therefore has nothing to do with the life of the author.

During the 50 year period in which copyright subsists, whoever owns the copyright will be entitled to:

- regulate the use of the photograph (i.e. those rights set out in section 7 subject to the limitations set out in sections 12 and 15)
- and also be entitled to grant licenses/receive royalties for such use.
- After expiry of the 50 year period, copyright will cease to exist in the work and the photograph will be open to public use.

As a photographer it is essential for the financial viability and sustainability of your business for you to own and control the copyright to your work so that you can sell license for use thereof. The current copyright law, whilst blatantly discriminating against photographers, does offer some protection if correctly applied.

On the 29th of August 2013 the Minister of Trade and Industry, Dr. Rob Davies, published the National Policy on Intellectual Property for broader public comments. The process of re-evaluating and revising the current copyright act is underway. On the 27th July 2015 the Department of Trade and Industry (DTI) published the Copyright Amendment Bill in the Government Gazette No. 39028, Government Notice No. 646. Despite photographers petitioning the DTI for copyright reformation there were no proposed changes to the existing copyright law relative to photographers other than the addition of a new section, Section 21(3) stating:

Amendment of section 21 of Act 98 of 1978

25. Section 21 of the principal Act is hereby amended by the addition after subsection (2) of

the following subsection:

(3) Ownership of any copyright whose owner cannot be located, is unknown, or is deceased shall vest in the state: Provided that if the owner of such copyright is located at anytime, ownership of such copyright shall be conferred back to such owner.

The revision not only reinforces the existing discriminatory legislation but seeks to empower Government as the owner of Orphan Works empowering Government to commercialise these Orphan Works as the 'Copyright Owner'.

An artistic work is defined in the Copyright Act 98 of 1978 (as amended) Section 1 (1)(iii):

"artistic work" means, irrespective of the artistic quality thereof—

(a) *paintings, sculptures, drawings, engravings and photographs;*

To define a photograph as an artistic work and then subject it to different legislation to other artistic works is discriminatory.

The revision of the copyright act is still in process. Considering that the current law discriminates against photographers and painters of portraits, there is hope that during this process the current law will be brought in line with the United Nations Declaration of Human Rights and the Berne Convention, empowering you, as the creator of your works, to "*lead a dignified economic existence*".

In the mean time the solution is good business documentation.

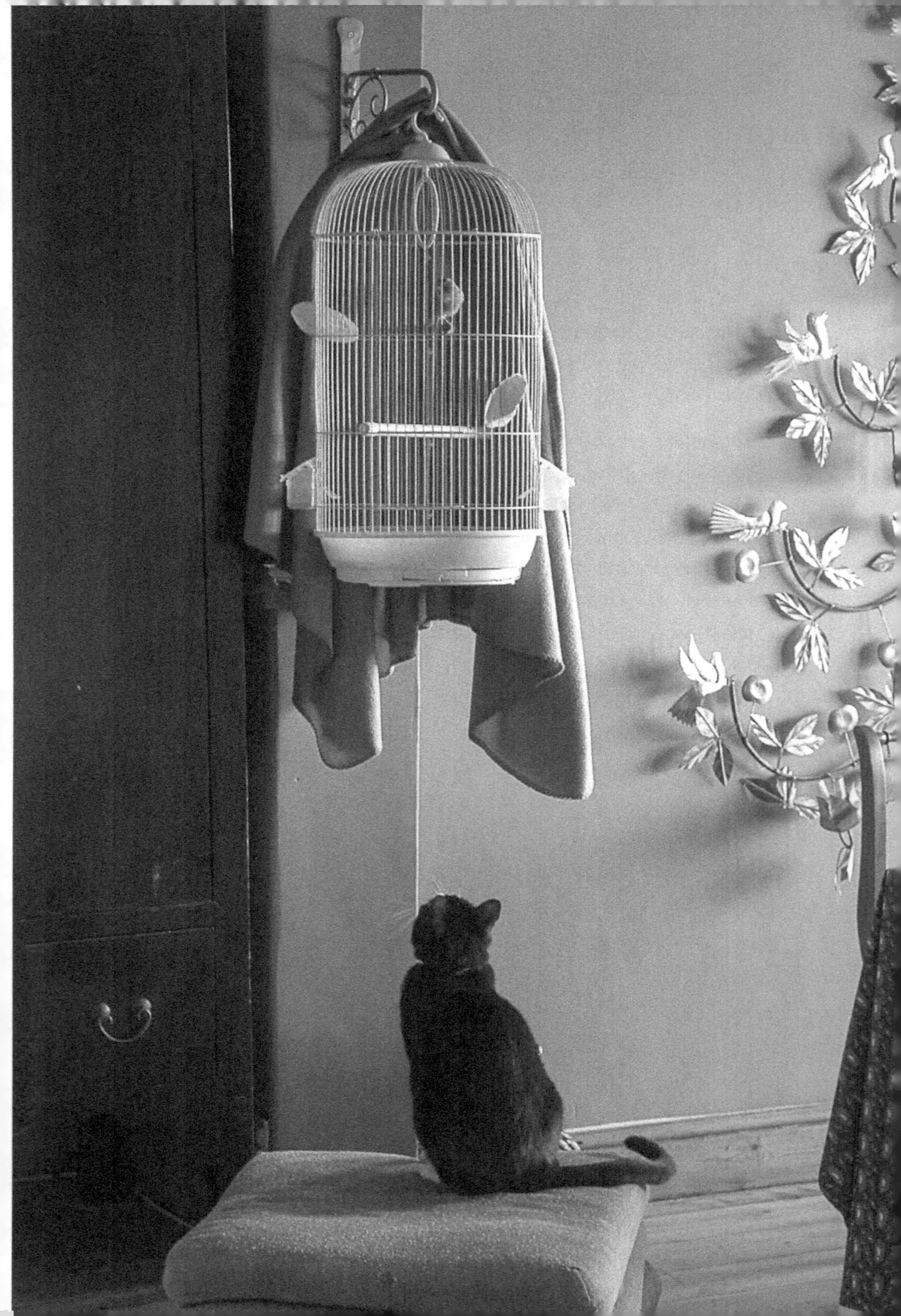

CHAPTER 5

THE PRIVACY RIGHT

"Look and think before opening the shutter. The heart and mind are the true lens of the camera."

Yousuf Karsh

The Privacy Right is the right to privacy concerning certain photographs and films.

Regardless of who owns the copyright to a work, people, and their property, displayed in the work have a Right to Privacy, especially around the financial exploitation of a photograph/film that they are featured in.

For the commercial use of a photograph/film the people featured in it must give their consent, preferably in writing, as a Model Release Form or a Release Form. This applies to private property as well that requires a Property Release Form signed by the owner of the property. Please note that the property owner, not the tenant, must sign a property release. In this case commercial use is defined as the use of photographs to promote or sell a product or service. Sample model and property releases are easily obtained from photo libraries or photographic associations like the Association of Photographers (AoP) or American Society of Media Photographers (ASMP). Model and property releases should specify the use of the images as well as the other required details.

Model and property releases are not required for EDITORIAL photography even though the photographer will benefit commercially from the sale of his/her photographs to editorial publications. By definition an editorial photograph is a photograph that illustrates an accompanying story, or in the case of a pictorial is a series of photographs that tell a story, usually accompanied by captions.

Except for Strategic Installations (National Key-points Act) anyone can be photographed anywhere remembering peoples right to privacy. There are places in which a person's right to privacy is a reasonable assumption like public toilets, hospitals and peoples homes. 'Fair use' includes news, works of art, satire, politics, informational or educational purposes, for which you don't need a person's consent.

Photographing buildings from a public place does not infringe copyright of the architect(s) who designed the building, nor owner of the building. Using buildings in the background of an image is legal if shooting from a public place but a permit from the local authority may be required for the shoot itself.

TRESPASS

There is currently no law in South Africa that prevents photographers from taking photographs on private property, however the law of trespass prevents or restricts access to private property.

Permission should always be obtained when photographing on or from private property. Many places appear to be public areas but are in fact privately owned, like the V&A Waterfront in Cape Town. Many of these centres display "Right of admission reserved" signs as well as other terms and conditions of entry, some listing photography as a prohibited activity. By entering the premises you consent to the terms and conditions.

Regardless of whether signs are displayed or not the property owner has the right to refuse access to the property and prevent photography. However, if no signs are displayed then it may be presumed that photography is allowed, until told otherwise by the centre management or security, who may prevent you from shooting in these spaces, and/or ask you to leave the premises. They may not, however, confiscate your camera equipment or force you to delete your images, nor may they delete your images themselves. This constitutes destruction of personal property.

Many of these centres will allow photography, with prior permission, some charging location fees for the privilege of shooting there. Should you be caught mistakenly photographing on private property you are likely to be charged with trespassing. An apologetic, cooperative approach to dealing with security officials goes a long way to ensuring no criminal charges are laid against you.

There are usually terms and conditions of entry attached to venues that charge an entrance fee such as theme parks, live performances, parties, museums or sports grounds. The ticket serves as the binding contract that you enter into when you purchase the ticket. Permits to shoot at these venues are normally obtainable from the venue management or event organiser or their appointed agent ahead of time, sometimes with royalty, or image supply conditions attached, normally on a 'take it or leave it' basis'.

Certain municipalities, and other governing bodies such as the South African National Parks, have bylaws that control or restrict photography in certain places. Permits can, and should, be applied for to shoot in these areas and all conditions of the permit complied with at all times.

The saying, *"Take nothing but photographs, leave nothing but footprints, kill nothing but time,"* runs deep and true.

Whilst you can photograph anyone or anything in, or from, a public place, and the act of taking a photograph is legal, there are exceptions being strategic installations or national key points. The use, not the content, of the photograph determines whether you need peoples, or the owner of properties, consent. Accessing private properties, without consent, is trespassing and is illegal.

TRADE MARKS

The *Trade Marks Act of 1993 (Act 194/1993)* regulates trade marks in South Africa.

A trade mark is a mark which distinguishes the same kind of goods or services of different parties. A 'mark' is defined by the act as *"any sign capable of being represented graphically, including a device, name, signature, word, letter, numeral, shape, configuration, pattern, ornamentation, colour or container for goods or any combination of the aforementioned"*.

Whilst the photographing of a trade mark is not an infringement in itself, the context in which the photograph is used may be, especially if used for advertising. The trade mark must be registered in South Africa, or in the country in which the photograph is shown, in order for it to be infringed. It is always advisable to remove all trademarks from images being used for advertising use, unless the advert is for the company, or person, who owns the trade mark. It is essential to remove trade marks from images you submit to a photo library as you have little or no control over who purchases the image and what it is used for.

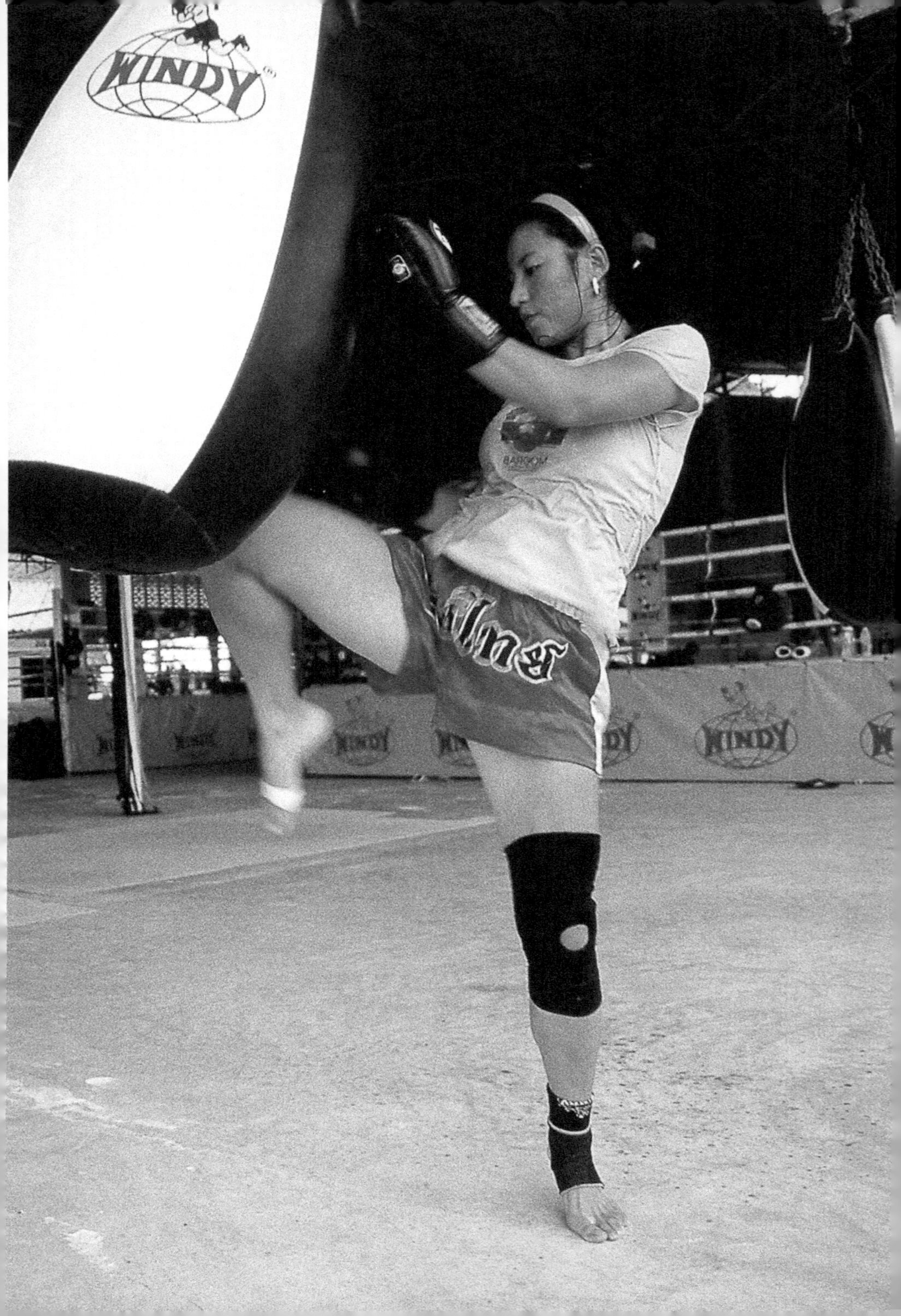
WINDY
WINDY
WINDY

CHAPTER 6

NATIONAL KEY POINTS / STRATEGIC INSTALLATIONS

"The only rules that really matter are these: what a man can do and what a man can't do."

Captain Jack Sparrow

The National Key Points Act, 1980 (Act No. 102 of 1980) is an act of Parliament that provides for the declaration and protection of sites of national strategic importance against sabotage.

National Key Points or Strategic Installations are places that the government determines to be important enough to the well being of the country to be protected and restrict access and activities to.

The National Key Points Act was originally implemented by the apartheid government under the guise of protection from terrorism, to secretly protect primarily privately owned strategic sites. Unfortunately the current government uses it at its convenience. Whilst protection from acts of terrorism is essential the loosely worded act gives the government broad sweeping powers open to its interpretation.

"*I am reminded about George Orwell's Animal Farm published in 1945. At the end, the past perpetrators of oppression and the revolutionaries who come to power are indistinguishable. Yet, how quickly, brazenly and unapologetically the ruling party uses an act it would have despised and rejected before, and rightly so, to shield its embarrassment and do damage control. Using a past law that does not even have a veneer of transparency, accountability or constitutionality devalues our constitution. The strategic abuse of the National Key Points Act is visibly and nakedly an abuse of office. It is regressive and objectionable. Only those who are morally bankrupt will use the old act as it is.*" Mosiuoa Lekota, COPE leader, former ANC member and former

Minister of Defence during a Parliamentary debate on the act in November 2013.

Prior to 2015 the government claimed that it was not obliged to publicly disclose the details of sites that have been declared National Key Points. In 2012 the Right2Know Campaign, and in 2013 the Democratic Alliance Parliamentary Opposition, demanded the government disclose a list of National Key Points. The Department of Police refused claiming they were acting in the interests of state security. Their refusal was appealed to the Johannesburg High Court, which ordered the government to release the list. On 22 January 2015 the government abandoned its attempt to appeal the ruling.

The list of 204 National Key Points was released by the Ministry of Police on the 16th January 2015 as follows:

NKP LIST 2015-01-16[4]

EASTERN CAPE (EC)

1. EC SABC PE
2. EC Grassridge Transmission Station, Addo
3. EC SA Reserve Bank, Port Elizabeth
4. EC SA Reserve Bank, East London
5. EC SABC Bhisho
6. EC EC Provincial Legislature
7. EC Oil Tanking Grinrod Caluto (Ltd) Port of Ngqura
8. EC Former Pres Res NR Mandela Qunu Village

[4] http://www.r2k.org.za/wp-content/uploads/List-of-National-Key-Points.pdf

FREE STATE (FS)

9. FS Vaaldam
10. FS Natref
11. FS Petronet Pump Station, Bethlehem
12. FS Coalbrook Petrol Pump Station
13. FS Sasol Pump Station
14. FS Perseus Transmission Station
15. FS Centlec Pty (Ltd) Electricity Distribution Station
16. FS SABC Freestate (BFN)
17. FS Kroonstad Pump Station
18. FS Lethabo Power Station
19. FS SA Reserve Bank, Bloemfontein
20. FS Provincial Legislature. Bloemfontein
21. FS Magdala TPL Depot
22. FS Wilge TPL Depot
23. FS/NC Hydra Transmission Station
24. FS/NC SABC Kimberley Northern Cape
25. FS/NC Square Kilometer Array Site (SKA)
26. FS/NC NC Provincial Legislature

GAUTENG (GN)

27. GN Onderstepoort Biological Products Ltd.
28. GN Union Buildings Presidency
29. GN Mahlambandlovu Pres Res
30. GN Setako Makgatho Presidential Res
31. GN OR Tambo International airport
32. GN SSA Communication Centre
33. GN Main Telephone Exchange (PPR)
34. GN Apoilo Transmission Station
35. GN Minerva Transmission Station
36. GN SA Bank Note Company

37. GN Denel Dynamics
38. GN Pretoria Metal Pressing
39. GN Pretoria Metal Pressing Pta West
40. GN Denel Land Systems Lyttetton
41. GN CSIR Wind Tunnel
42. GN SA Post Office Computer Centre
43. GN SA Reserve Bank HQ
44. GN SA Reserve Bank: Pta North
45. GN New Cooperation Building ID Factory
46. GN SABC Tshwane
47. GN SITA Numerus Building
48. GN SITA Centurion
49. GN Denel Integrated System Solutions
50. GN SITA Beta
51. GN Government Printing Works (Sec Print Facility)
52. GN Waltloo TPL Depot
53. GN/NW Transnet Pipeline Rustenburg Depot
54. GN/NW North West Prov Legislature
55. GN/NW Hartebeeshoek Earth Station
56. GN/NW NECSA
57. GN/NW SA National Space Agency (SANSA)
58. GN/NW SABC Lt North West
59. GS Rheinmetall Denel Munition
60. GS SABC Building, Aucland Park
61. GS Sentech Tower in Brixton, Johannesburg
62. GS SENTECH Transmission Satellite Centre
63. GS Office of Interception Centres
64. GS Eskom National Control Centre, Simmerpan
65. GS City Power Johannesburg Pty (Ltd)
66. GS Grootvlei Power Station
67. GS Former Pres Res NR Mandela GP

68. GS Former, Pres Res T Mbeki GP
69. GS Pres Residence of SA GP
70. GS Gauteng Provincial Legislature
71. GS ArcelorMittal
72. GS African Explosives Ltd.
73. GS NCP Chlorchem, Chloorkop, Kempton Park
74. GS Denel Aviation
75. GS BAE Systems Benoni
76. GS SA Mint
77. GS SA Reserve Bank, Johannesburg
78. GS Shetl Depot Alrode
79. GS Chevron Alrode
80. GS Sasol Depot Alrode
81. GS Total Depot
82. GS Transnet Pipeline: Alrode
83. GS Chevron Texaco
84. GS Transnet Pipeline: Airport
85. GS e-Natis Facility
86. GS Rand Water: Zwartkopjies
87. GS Rand Water: Zuikerbosch
88. GS Rand Water: Vereeniging
89. GS Rand Water: Maplteton
90. GS Rand Water: Barrage
91. GS Rand Water: Palmiet
92. GS Rand Water: Eikenhof
93. GS Transnet Pipeline Tarlton Distribution Depot
94. GS Klerksdorp Depot
95. GS Langleagte Depot
96. GS Vaaldam Pump Station
97. GS Meyerton Depot

KWAZULU NATAL (KZN)

98. KZN SABC Durban
99. KZN Total SA (Cutler)
100. KZN Acacia Operations Services (Heartland Leasing)
101. KZN Engen Depot (Cutter)
102. KZN Total Depot (Cutler)
103. KZN Valvoline Depot (Cutler)
104. KZN PD Terminals Depot (Cutler)
105. KZN Caleb Brett (Cutler)
106. KZN Industrial Oil Processors (Cutler)
107. KZN Durban Bulk Shipping (Cutler)
108. KZN SA Petroleum Refinery (SAPREF) (Cutler)
109. KZN SA Pretroleum Refinery (SAPREF) Reunion
110. KZN Engen Refinery
111. KZN Natcos (Cutler)
112. KZN Natcos
113. KZN Single Buoy Mooring
114. KZN Trensnet Pumping Station: Newcastle
115. KZN Impala Transmission Station
116. KZN Klaarwater Distribution Station
117. KZN Pegasus Transmission Station
118. KZN Drakensberg Power Station
119. KZN Island View Storage (Cutler)
120. KZN Caltex Depot (Cutler)
121. KZN Zenex Depot (Cutler)
122. KZN Durban South Distribution Station
123. KZN Transnet Pumping - Station: Ladysmith
124. KZN Transnet Pumping - Station: (Cutler)
125. KZN Transnet Pumping - Station: Quagga's Nek
126. KZN Transnat Pumping - Station: Hillcrest

127. KZN Transnet Pumping; Station: Howlck
128. KZN Transnet Pumping Station: Van Reenen
129. KZN Pres of SA Res - KZN
130. KZN Presidential Res - JL Dube House
131. KZN New Aviation Fuel Depot at KSIA
132. KZN King Shaka International Airport Air Side
133. KZN Durban North Distribution Station
134. KZN Athene TransmisSion Station
135. KZN Lotus Park Distribution station
136. KZN SA Reserve Bank: Durban
137. KZN Duzi TPL Depot
138. KZN Mooi River TPL Depot
139. KZN Fortmistake Transnet Pipeline Ladysmith
140. KZN Mngeni TPL Depot
141. KZN Mnambithi TPL Depot
142. KZN Ntwini TPL Depot
143. KZN Hilltop TPL Depot
144. KZN KZN Provincial Legislature

MPUMULANGA (MP)

145. MP Grootdraai Pumping Station
146. MP SABC Nelspruit
147. MP Camden Power Station
148. MP Hendrina Power Station
149. MP Kriel Power Station
150. MP Arnot Power Station
151. MP Sol Transmission Station
152. MP Matte Power Station
153. MP Duvha Power Station
154. MP Tutuka Power Station
155. MP Kendal Power Station

156. MP Komati Power Station
157. Majuba Power Station
158. MP Mpumalanga Boulevard Riverside Gov Building Nelspruit
159. MP Transnet Pipeline, Kendal
160. MP Sasol Secunda
161. MP Transnet Pipelines, Secunda
162. MP Jericho Pump Station
163. MP Rieftontein Pump Station
164. MP Grootfontein Pump Station
165. MP Vygeboom Pump Station
166. MP Bosloop Water Pump Station
167. MP Nooitgedact Pump Station
168. MP Transnet Pipeline Witbank Depot
169. MP Khutala Pump Station
170. MP Zaaihoek Pump Station
171. MP Knoppies Tower
172. MP/LIM SABC, Polokwane
173. Mokolo Pump Station, Limpopo Prov
174. MP/LIM Matimba Power Station
175. MP/LIM Limpopo Legislature, Lebowakgomo, Polokwane

WESTERN CAPE (WC)

176. WC Parliament House
177. WC 120 Plain Street, Capetown
178. WC Cape Town international Airport
179. WC SABC Ltd Western Cape
180. WC Chevron Refinery, Cape Town
181. WC Saldanha Tank Farm
182. WC Muldersviai Transmission Station

183. WC Acasia Transmission Station
184. WC Droeriver Transmission Station
185. WC Koeberg Nuclear Power Station
186. WC RDM Somerset West
187. WC RDM Weliington
188. WC PetroSA Voorbaai
189. WC SA Reserve Bank, Cape Town
190. WC PetroSA GTL Refinery
191. WC Single buoy mooring Voorbaai
192. WC Klipheuwel Pumping Station
193. WC FA Production Platform, Mossgas
194. WC Orca
195. WC Presidential Res (Genadendal)
196. WC Former Pres Res FW de Klerk (Sea Point)
197. WC Former Pres Res NR Mandela (Bishops Court)
198. WC Office of the Pres of SA (Tuynhuys)
199. WC SABC : Air Time :Cape Town
200. WC Western Cape Provincial Legislature
201. WC Gourikwa Power Station
202. WC SFF Association Storage
203. WC Ankerlig Power Station
204. WC SFF Oil Jetty

Photography is listed as a prohibited activity of and around these installations.

A member of the SAPS, charged with safety and security in the RSA, can refuse you permission to photograph State owned property claiming protection under this vague Act. Whilst photojournalists have been recently arrested and detained under this act the charges have been dropped. If arrested under this act, the SAPS may confiscate a photographers camera equipment as evidence, for which they must issue a property receipt. The photographic equipment must be returned if the charges are dropped.

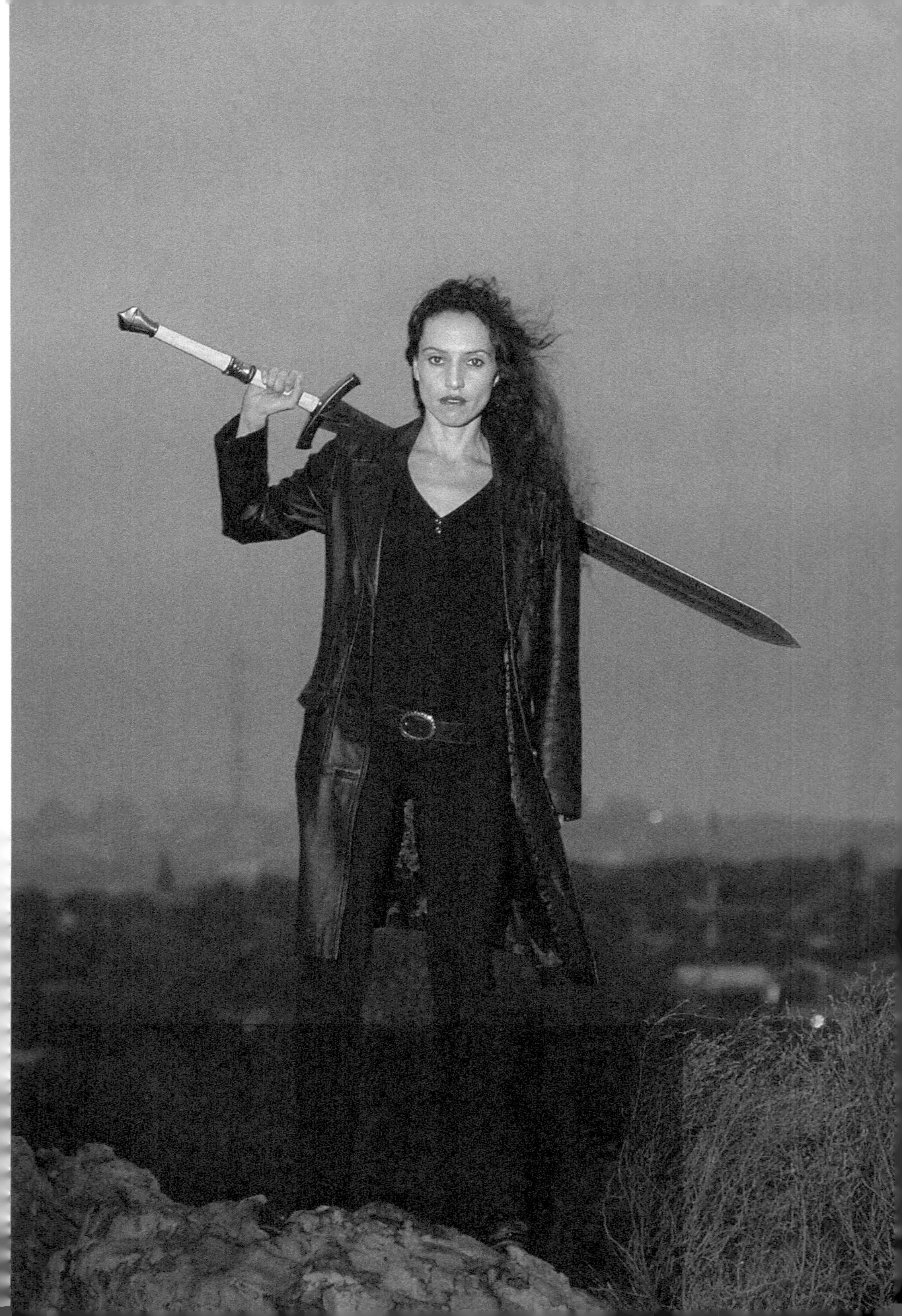

CHAPTER 7

CONTRACTS

"I have every faith in your reconciliatory navigational skills, Master Gibbs. Now where is that monkey? I want to shoot something!"

Captain Jack Sparrow

South Africa has a hybrid legal system, a combination of a number of legal traditions:

- A *Civil Law* system inherited from the Dutch,
- A *Common Law* system inherited from the British
- A *Customary Law* system inherited from indigenous Africans (African Customary Law).

Generally, South Africa follows English law in the areas of procedural law, company law and the law of evidence. Roman-Dutch common law is followed in contract law, law of delict (tort), law of persons, law of things and family law.

The implementation of the New Constitution in 1997 added to this. *Constitutional Law* is the highest law of the land and supersedes all other laws.

South African contract law is a version of the Roman-Dutch law of contract, which is rooted in Roman law.

A contract is an agreement entered into willingly by two or more parties with contractual capacity, which is legal, physically possible, complies with the required formalities, with the serious intention of creating a legal obligation that results in rights and duties.

THE LAW OF CONTRACT

The law of contract is the body of legal rules governing the conclusion and consequences of contracts. It defines the basis and requirements of contractual liability, as well as the rights and duties of the parties. It regulates the breach of contract and provides remedies for it, and it governs the termination of contractual obligations. RSA law defines obligations generally, assigning categories only to transactions that occur often.

A legal obligation is a legal tie between legal subjects, recognised by law, which is created as a result of a certain legal fact and which creates rights and duties that are recognised by law. A legal obligation consists of two elements, namely the right of the creditor to claim performance and the duty of the debtor to perform accordingly. The creditor's right is known as a personal right, which corresponds to the legal object of performance (i.e. a specific action or inaction, delivery of a specific thing or payment of a specific amount of money).

Contracts are civil obligations in which the rights and duties are recognised and enforced by law.

In order for a contract to be valid and binding the following requirements must be met:

- There must be consensus between the contracting parties. A conscious agreement must be made with genuine concurrent intention.
- The parties must have the capacity to contract, in other words they must be legally capable of concluding a binding contract.
- The agreement must be legal and may not contradict a statutory or common law rule.
- The contract must abide by any formalities set by law or by the parties themselves.

- The performance of the obligations must be possible.
- Contractual parties are required to conduct their relationship in good faith or *bona fides*.

The law presumes that every person has *contractual capacity*. In some people the capacity to conclude valid contracts is either lacking or limited such as minors, the insane, insolvent persons, prodigals, and those intoxicated by drink or drugs.

The validity of a contract does not generally depend on compliance with any formalities. Some types of contracts are required by law to be in writing, registered, or notarially executed, such as the sale of land, and assignment of copyright and suretyships.

Remember that every contract is an agreement willingly entered into. Every contract is negotiable and we all have the right to walk away from an agreement that is not in our best interests. Every contract should contain an exit clause that specifies how the contract may be terminated.

One of the areas of danger in contracts today is agreements that we enter into on the internet, such as software license agreements or terms and conditions of use of web sites or social networks. By ticking the box 'I agree' you are consenting to the terms of the contract and are bound by it. How many of us actually read the terms before ticking 'I agree'?

There are a number of web sites, social networks and photographic competitions that rely on this and include terms that grant them license to use your photographs, with the right to sub-license and sell your images, with no payment to you, holding you liable for the use of the images, that you have no control over.

Perhaps it's time for us to read contracts before we sign them and to walk away from the ones that are unfair. Many web sites and social networks are thinly disguised content libraries that collect and sub license your images and videos, holding you liable for other peoples use thereof.

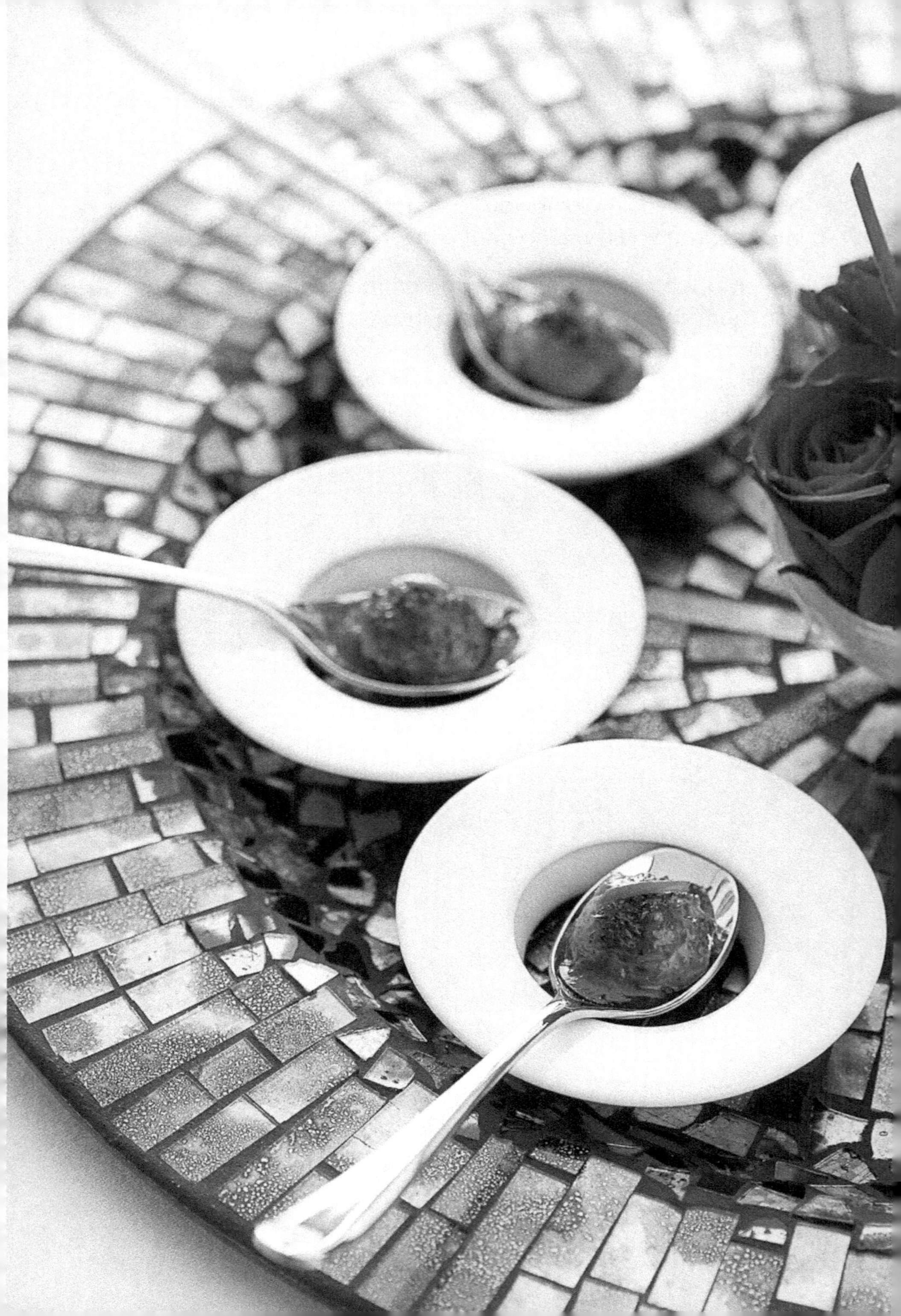

CHAPTER 8

HOW MUCH SHOULD I CHARGE?

"Ah-ha! So, we've established my proposal as sound in principle. Now, we're just haggling over price."

Captain Jack Sparrow

This is the question of all questions and the one I hear the most. "How much should I charge?" The answer is quite simple. Anything you want to. South Africa is a free market system based on willing buyer/willing seller. You can ask any price you want to and if your client is prepared to pay it, you have a deal. There are no prescribed rates for photography.

As a young emerging pro I struggled to understand why there are different base usage rates for different markets of photography. I used the Professional Photographers of South Africa (PPSA) Price and Usage Guide that specified recommended rates. When asking why the 'Advertising, Creative, Fashion & Beauty' rate was R10 500/day and the 'Aerial, Architectural, Commercial, Industrial & Mining rate was R8 500/day[5], I was told things like the 'first category is more creative' and 'has a higher financial value to the end user'. I wanted to know what the rates were based on, how they had been calculated and no-one I spoke to knew the answer. With a five year background in construction this concerned me. In construction the reputable construction companies place a lot of emphasis on calculating and monitoring actual costs to ensure that their projects are financially viable. Why did photographers not do the same? The argument that advertising photography requires a greater level of creative input is nonsense to me. We should invest the same level of creative input into every job we do, regardless of it's use.

---

[5] Rates quoted from the 2007 PPSA Price & Usage Guide

I now know that the true value of photography is not in how much you charge per day, it's in owning the intellectual property to your work empowering you to sell license for use thereof. Your day rate must make financial sense, in that it must be financially viable, but the danger with day rates is that you are selling time. When you're not shooting you're not earning. Selling the license for use of your work means that your images are working for you, even if you're not shooting.

So the big question should actually be, "How much should I charge in order to have a financially viable and sustainable career as a professional photographer?"

In advertising this is known as your 'charge out rate' or 'day rate'.

CALCULATING YOUR OVERHEADS (FIXED COSTS)

The calculation of your overheads is a basic business costing. It is essential to do this in order to determine how much you should charge, in order to have a financially viable and sustainable career.

A financially viable and sustainable career means a career in which you earn enough money in order to:

- draw a salary every month
- afford medical insurance and retirement provision
- pay your bills when they are due
- take paid annual and sick leave
- purchase and maintain the required equipment
- make a profit (return on your investment).

First, calculate your total business overheads.

Then determine what salary, with benefits, you would like to earn (gross, before tax).

Add your profit margin to this and divide by the average number of shoot days per month you anticipate.

DAY RATE CALCULATOR	
	Per Month
Accounting Fees & Part-time Book Keeper	1,045.00
Advertising & Marketing (Portfolio, Z-Cards, adverts)	1,375.00
Bank charges	385.00
Cellphone - Photographer	935.00
Cellphone - Assistant's allowance	385.00
Competition entry fees	385.00
Computer Expenses	1,375.00
Consumables (Cleaning products etc)	550.00
Continued Professional Development	1,493.80
Courier	330.00
Depreciation (excluding DCF depreciation)	4,583.70
Electricity & Water	385.00
Entertainment	1,650.00
Equipment (Excluding digital camera equipment)	4,583.70
Equipment repairs and maintenance	550.00
Insurance - Life/Accident/Disability	770.00
Insurance - General/Premises/Equipment/Liability	1,094.50
Legal Fees (Provision)	550.00
Lunches & refreshments	220.00
Medical Aid - Photographer	1,485.00
Motor Vehicle Expenses - Repayment/Finance	3,300.00
Motor Vehicle Expenses - Maintenance	1,650.00
Motor Vehicle Expenses - Fuel & oil	3,575.00
Printing & Stationery	330.00
Rent - Studio/Office	13,200.00
Repairs and maintenance - Studio/Office	1,650.00
Salaries & Wages (Cleaner/Assistant)	9,900.00
Security (Armed response)	330.00
Telephone	550.00

Web site hosting	110.00
The Murphy Factor (Other "Train Smash" incidentals)	550.00

Overheads Summary

Total monthly overheads	59,275.70
Total annual overheads (12 months)	711,308.40

GROSS monthly salary to live on (for yourself!)	25,000.00

Average number of shoot days per month	10

RECOVERY REQUIRED 11 MNTI	**Daily**	**Monthly**	**Yearly**
Overheads	6,466.44	64,664.40	711,308.40
Salary	2,727.27	27,272.73	300,000.00
Total GP required at cost	9,193.71	91,937.13	,011,308.40
Profit margin @ 25%	2,298.43		

DAY RATE REQUIRED	**11,492.14**
HOURLY RATE REQUIRED (8hrs)	**1,436.52**

Remember that the RECOVERY REQUIRED formula is based on anticipated actual shoot days being 11 months of the year, 10 days per month. By basing your formula on 11 months of the year you make provision for three weeks annual paid leave and one week paid sick leave.

The GROSS monthly salary to live on (for yourself) is the 'total cost to company', and includes PAYE, pension/ provident fund as well as all other applicable payroll deductions. It is NOT the photographer's 'take home' salary.

Many professional photographers struggle to understand why it is that they cannot afford to take annual leave, or make provision for retirement. The answer is quite simply that their day rate is too low and they are under-recovering their overheads with very little or no profit. As can be seen from the table above, for this particular commercial photographer's business, he/she must charge a minimum day rate of **R 11 492.14** to meet his/her financial obligations. This is assuming that the photographer is able to shoot 10 full days per month and *EXCLUDES* the photographers equipment, costed separately as a Digital Capture Fee. Considering that many commissioned bookings are only for half a day, this compounds the problem of recovering your overheads. There are on average 20.75 normal working days per month. Every shoot requires preproduction planning and organisation and post production. Achieving a goal of ten shoot (full) days per month leaves 10.75 days per month for preproduction, post production, marketing and administration.

There are negotiable and nonnegotiable parts to the day rate. The recovery of actual costs, including your salary, should be nonnegotiable. The only negotiable part is your profit margin. Whilst your profit margin is negotiable remember that it is essential to make profit to build up working capital reserves for rainy days, so ensure that you don't negotiate your profit margin too low!

In the costing example the photographer has and maintains their own studio premises, dedicated to their business. This is only possible if commanding day rates that can carry the cost of the studio. Most photographers in South Africa's day rates are too low to carry the cost of a dedicated studio and either rent their studio out or use hire studios. The advantage of hire studios is that you don't carry the cost of the studio if you're not shooting in studio. Many editorial clients, who pay the lowest base usage rates, demand that photographers have their own studio. Some publishers pay a nominal day rate fee for 'studio rental' that seldom covers what rental studios charge. Considering that publishers pay the lowest base usage rates, even if they do pay a nominal studio day rate, it is highly unlikely that it will cover the operating costs of a photographer's own studio, leaving the photographer to subsidise the publisher for that day.

The truth is that you are paying a client to work for them if you charge less than your required day rate as you are running at a loss for that day. You have to make up this loss from somewhere else, normally your salary and/or benefits. Considering that we are in business to make profit, I can only wonder why photographers want to pay clients to work for them.

25% operating profit, as a percentage of gross revenue, is deemed by the Advertising Industry to be a "fair agency profit".

The Advertising Industry is a service industry and operates under conditions of unusual risk and uncertainty. A 25% operating profit is lower than other comparable businesses, such as lawyers, contractors, management consultants and accountants, who generally aim to achieve an operating profit closer to 33.3%.

Like an advertising agency, professional photography is a service business that also operates under conditions of unusual risk and uncertainty, and is also entitled to a "fair profit". A "fair profit" for professional photography is therefore between 25-33%. South Africa is a free market system based on willing buyer, willing seller. As such you can charge any profit margin you want to and if your client is willing to pay it then you have a deal.

Half day rates should be charged at 60% of the applicable full day rate with a maximum of half of the stipulated time period.

Whilst some advertising agencies work on hourly rates it is seldom in a photographer's best interests to charge on an hourly basis due to set up and wrap up time requirements, that are chargeable. As such photographers day rates are normally charged in full or half day increments.

It is challenging for photographers in South Africa to command the day rates we need in order to have a financially viable and sustainable career. Many photographers end up subsidising their clients, to their own detriment. One of the solutions to this is charging USAGE. By charging usage, through selling the license for use of an image, a photographer can earn extra income from the same shoot by selling extended license for use if the client requires it at a later stage, topping up the initial shortfall the photographer made at the time of the shoot.

CHARGING ON A RATE PER PICTURE SUPPLIED BASIS

This is another of those million dollar, frequently asked, how long is a piece of string questions. Many photographers build up their own image libraries and sell individual images instead of charging for a shoot on a 'Day Rate' basis. The question being, "How much should I charge for the license for use of my image?" Remember, photographers do not sell time nor photographs, we sell license for use of our intellectual property, the physical manifestation of which is the photograph. Bearing this in mind it is advisable to never sell individual images but to rather sell the license for use of the images, either on an exclusive or non-exclusive basis. Determining the value of the sale of an individual photograph for commercial use is a mine field as clients can buy a royalty free image from a micro stock agency for 1 US$, up to many thousand US$ for a rights managed image. Positioning yourself in this market is based on a number of key points being:

- The originality of the image - Are there many similar images available or is yours truly unique?
- Whether you are selling exclusive or non-exclusive license for use of the image.
- How many times the image has been sold before.
- What uses has the image been used for before and by who? Advertisers are wary of using the same images bought by their competing brands.

A simple method for determining the starting point of the value of the image is to calculate your total production costs for the creation of the images and divide that by the number of final images for that day resulting in an actual cost per image. The total production cost includes all of the related expenses such as model, location and support crew fees, equipment hire (whether hired from a company or yourself), catering, transport, retouching as well as any other costs associated with the shoot day.

For example:

8 final shots created at a total production cost of R43 000,00

R43 000,00 / 8 = R5 375,00 per image.

Based on this you are then able to negotiate the fee per use of the image knowing what the actual production cost of the image is. It is strongly recommended that you only sell the license to use your images on a Rights Managed basis. This means that you sell the license for use of each image with clear terms as to what the image may be used for including the time period, territories and media.

It is common for image libraries like Gallo Images, Getty Images and Corbis Images to charge different rates for different uses. Editorial rates are often determined by the size the image is used as well as the location it is used. A cover image commands a higher fee than an image used as a quarter page in an editorial feature. Using the image for advertising use usually commands the highest fee.

Exclusive use of the image commands a high fee as it negates the possibility of selling the image to another buyer during the time period of the license, whereas non-exclusive use means that the license to use the same image can be sold to many different buyers for varied uses at the same time.

You can determine the value of the image to you by calculating the actual production cost and estimating the number of times the image is likely to sell and for what uses. At best this is a guestimate but with time and experience patterns will emerge that you can use for more accurate calculations in future.

Remember to always specify your Base Usage Rate when supplying Cost Estimates for the license for use of images to ensure that it is recorded up front should extended use be required at a later stage.

Alternatively, in order to determine an accurate market related value, search for images similar to yours on reputable image libraries like Getty Images www.gettyimages.com or Corbis Images www.corbisimages.com, using their price calculator select the RM (Rights Managed) option, select the applicable uses being the territory (country), time period and media (web/print etc) and determine what they would charge for the use of the image. You can then base the sale of your image on this information, setting your price within this ballpark. Getty Images Rights Managed calculator can be found at http://www.gettyimages.com/pricecalculator/sb10069475ab-001. This calculator considers the following factors:

1. Image Usage (the media the image will be used in)

2. Usage Specs (circulation figures and time period)
3. Target Market (territories the image will be used in as well as for which industries)

The calculator is simple to use provided you have the correct information from your client. If not then you need to check the requirements for determining the value of the image and request these details for use from your client BEFORE providing them with the price to buy the license for use of the image.

The price for the license for use determined by the online calculator is a good indiction of what your image is worth and provides an excellent basis for you to negotiate the fee from.

Remember that images with releases (model and property releases) have a higher value than unreleased images as released images can be sold for advertising purposes whilst unreleased images can only really be sold for editorial purposes.

Many stock photographers start out by using their family and friends as models and their properties for locations, in order to secure releases whilst not paying a fortune in model and location fees. Whilst this does save money and help to get you on the road you will quickly discover that working with professional models is often a lot quicker and easier as they understand what the photographer needs and perform accordingly. Models are in essence actors, performing the role required of them to create a scene or mood and often understand how to move and behave to look their best for camera.

Model agencies are quite often reluctant to allow their models to model for photo libraries as they are unable to control how long, and for what uses, the images are used for. This often conflicts with campaigns their models are employed for once they are established. As such model agencies will often put forward their 'new faces' in need of experience and portfolio material for photo library shoots.

Remember that for location releases, the owner of the property or their appointed agent needs to sign the release, not the tenant.

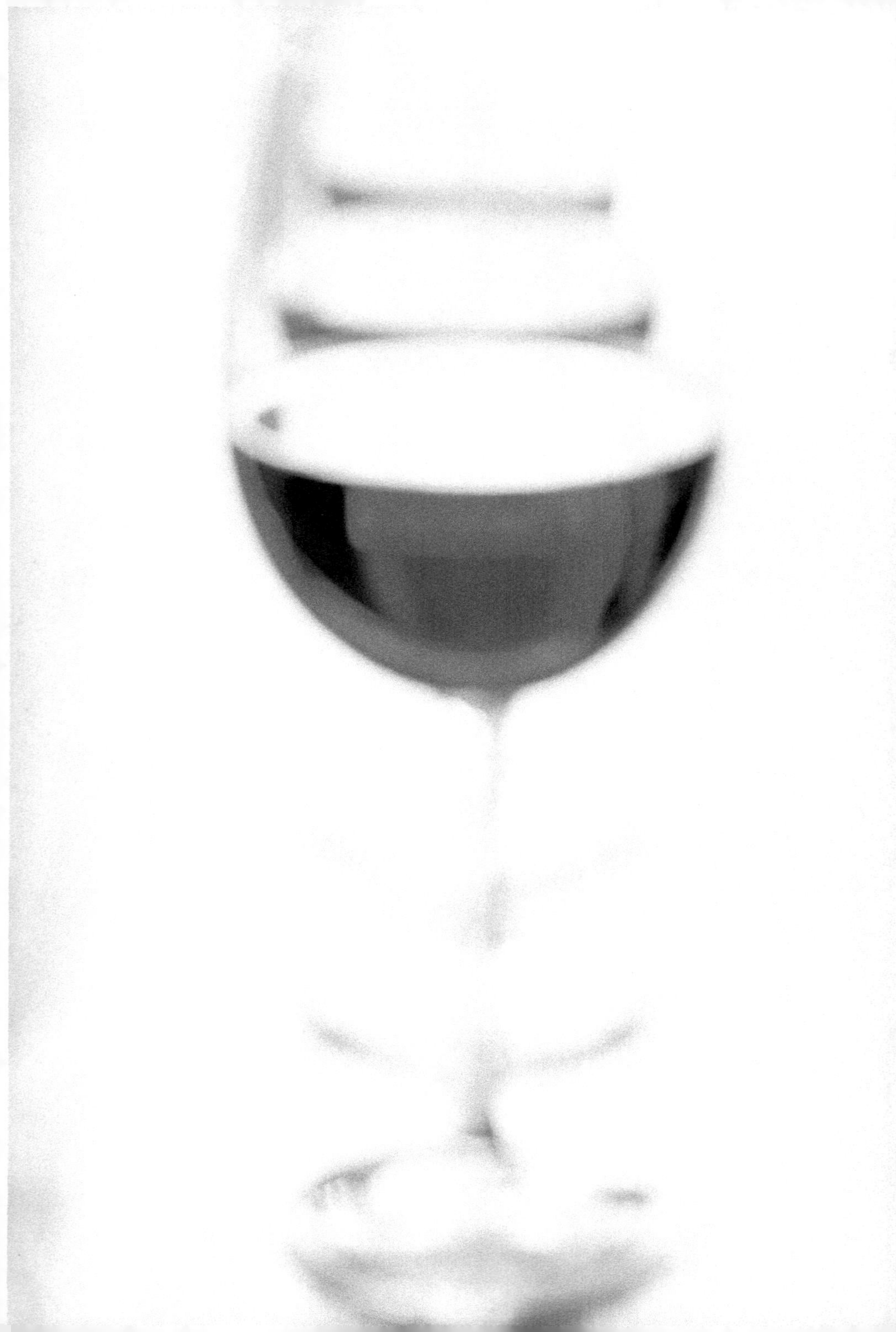

CHAPTER 9

BASE USAGE RATES (BUR)

"There are always two people in every picture: the photographer and the viewer."

Ansel Adams

The Base Usage is the primary use for which the creation of an image is commissioned and is limited to use within the borders of the Republic of South Africa (one territory), for one year, in two media, or two years in one media, or once off use in one edition in the case of editorial use.

A Base Usage Rate can, and should, be established for images sold individually, from a photographer's archive or image library as well.

Base Usage Rates (BUR) include the photographer's overheads and creative fee but exclude specialised camera equipment (including digital), lighting, studio, materials and production costs. These should be recorded separately in the cost estimate, as required.

The use of images commissioned by the client should transfer to the client on receipt of full and final payment, with the use of the images specific to the purpose the images were commissioned for.

The Base Usage Rates (BUR) are allocated time constraints for the sake of ease of management, a standard day being nine hours, that allows for a one hour break for lunch. Editorial days are based on an eight hour day, including lunch.

The BUR is based on the use of the image(s) in South Africa only. Should the images be used outside of South Africa then the photographer is entitled to charge the applicable usage.

The BUR consists of the photographer's day rate and creative fee combined. Photographers creative fees will differ according to their level of expertise and experience, as will their overheads. As such photographers BURs will differ from one another. These differences in rates can be confusing to a client who requests a number of photographers to price a job. Your thorough understanding of how you calculated your BUR will assist you to motivate it to your client.

Although it is a photographer's legal, moral right to be named as the Author of their work, the byline (image credit to photographer) is perceived to have a financial value as it serves as advertising for the photographer, hence the reduced BUR rates for advertorial and editorial shoots. Should an image be used for either advertorial or editorial use without a byline published clearly visible next to the image, then the photographer is entitled to charge their full commercial fee as compensation.

BUYOUTS BASED ON BASE USAGE RATES (BUR)

The BUR was established to assist photographers and clients determine a base value for photographic work that can be used when determining buyout values for further usage of images.

It is suggested that the minimum BUR should be the equivalent of the calculated day rate. Whilst the photographers creative fee should be added to this, at the very least costs will be covered.

If a photographer agrees to lower his/her rate in consideration of a client's budget constraints it is strongly recommended that the normal BUR be listed on the Cost Estimate and that the normal BUR be used when estimating buy outs, if they occur at a later stage. A line can be added indicating the discount given, such as "Less budget consideration" with the discount deducted from the listed BUR.

The standard BUR is based on once-off use in one territory, for one year, or in the case of editorial commissions, once off use in one publication only.

In Advertising the BUR is based on use in two media, in one territory, for one year OR one media, in one territory, for two years only. The time and media are interchangeable, the territory is not.

BUYOUTS / REUSE

Buyouts/usage is an internationally recognised and accepted principle. Similar principles that govern the modelling industry apply to photographers too.

Buyouts are based on three factors being:

1) Types of **MEDIA** the image is to be used in.
2) The length of **TIME** exclusive use is assigned.
3) The **TERRITORY** in which the image will be used.

Just as Microsoft requires a license for every new installation (use) of their software, so are photographers entitled to charge for every use of their images. The extended use of a photographer's intellectual property directly and proportionately increases the client's sales of the products or services represented in the images.

The Association of Photographers (AOP) Re-usage Calculator is highly recommend should you need assistance with calculating usage value.[6] Each additional territory, time and media has a calculated value. The larger the territory, in terms of buying power, the higher the value. The usage for principle media for the United States of America is 200% of the BUR whilst Asia (excluding Japan) is only 75%.

Buyouts are common practice in advertising photography but less common in Corporate/Design and Editorial photography. Standard use of editorial photographs is once off use in one edition of the publication. Should the publication publish a second edition or want to reuse an image they should buy the rights to do so.

Sometimes clients want images that are shot for Advertorial/Promotions purposes in a publication to be used for advertising. The simplest way of calculating the 'upgrade' fee for this is to charge the difference between the Advertorial fee paid and the photographer's Advertising fee, thereby 'upgrading' the use to advertising, empowering the client to use any of the images created on that day for advertising purposes. Remember that if models are included in the images, their use will have to be upgraded with their model agency too, in order to release the images for advertising use.

[6] http://www.the-aop.org/information/usage-calculator

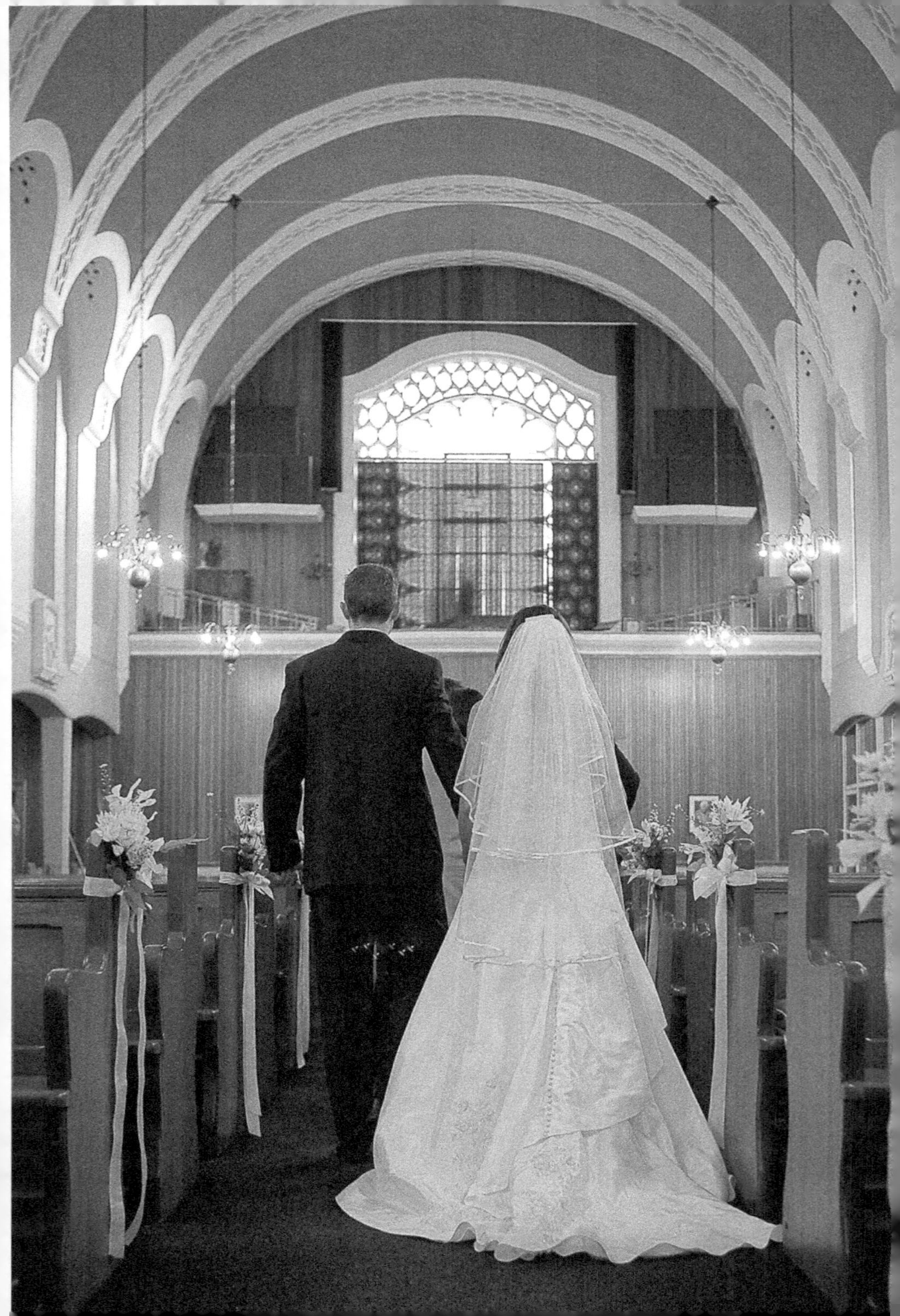

CHAPTER 10

DIGITAL CAPTURE FEES (DCF)

"Twelve significant photographs in any one year is a good crop."

Ansel Adams

DIGITAL CAPTURE FEES (DCF)

The Digital Capture Fee (DCF) was introduced to assist photographers with the recovery of their digital equipment overhead costs.

Digital photography has placed an enormous digital equipment overhead burden on photographers who have to supply the digital camera systems and accessories as well as the computer hardware and software necessary to complete their assignments. The speed with which technology improves means that photographers need to replace their digital systems approximately every three years to keep up with technological advancement.

Before digital photography clients paid for film, processing and scanning costs. The digital process has replaced this and the digital capture fee was introduced in its place to assist photographers to recoup their digital overhead costs. The Digital Capture Fee includes the camera equipment, computer hardware and software and digital accessories but does not include lighting, photographic assistant or any other costs. These should be costed separately in the photographer's cost estimate.

When shooting film, the photographer would take the exposed film to a lab for processing. The digital RAW files (CR2, NEF, DNG) are the equivalent of the exposed, unprocessed film. Just as exposed film required processing in a lab, digital RAW files require processing in a 'digital lab' such as Adobe Lightroom, Adobe Bridge, Apple Aperture or Capture One Pro. A photographer would never hand over exposed, unprocessed film to a client as certain corrections were made during processing such as clips and balances. Likewise a photographer should not hand over off camera RAW files to a client but should always process them first.

The DCF is made up of two parts. The first being the required fee to recover digital overheads. The second is to cover the photographer's time spent on editing and processing the digital images.

Editing and retouching are *NOT* the same thing. Editing is the process of selecting the final shots for use and converting these images from their RAW file format to the required output file, usually using software like Adobe Lightroom, Apple's Aperture or Capture One Pro. Retouching is the process of taking these output files and changing or altering them through digital manipulation, usually using software such as Adobe Photoshop.

The digital capture fee (DCF) covers image capture and digital editing & processing ONLY and does not include any form of retouching at all.

The capture rates for photographers using medium format digital should be three times those of photographers using a digital SLR due to the substantially higher equipment costs of medium format digital equipment.

There are wedding photographers who advertise packages that include 400, the most I've seen is 2 000 images, supplied to client. Not only does this tell me that the photographer has not done their costings properly, but is, in all likelihood, a bad photographer. Considering that a wedding album doesn't normally hold more than

80-100 photographs, what is any client going to do with 400, let alone 2 000 photographs! A good photographer is likely to supply about 50% of the images that they shoot to the client for final selection, after the first edit. This means that in order to supply 2 000 images the photographer has to shoot 4 000 images, unless they're supplying the client with almost everything they shoot.

When shooting 35mm film, a wedding photographer was likely to shoot an average of five rolls of 36 exposure film totalling 180 images, guaranteeing 80-100 final images to the client. Fewer considered shots create better images, less work and lower long term overheads than machine gun shooting.

CALCULATING YOUR DCF

The calculation of your Digital Capture Fee (DCF), also known as a capture rate, is made up of three main parts:

1. Calculate the cost of your photographic equipment.
2. Add your insurance, an allowance for repairs and maintenance, depreciation and your profit margin to this.
3. Add the time it takes to download the images to your computer, edit them (including basic corrections) and export the final 'off camera' images to their required file format.

The following table is an example of the start up equipment requirements for a professional photographer. The equipment chosen is not the top of the range professional equipment but rather current, good quality, professional entry level equipment that can be built on.

It is essential for you as a photographer to calculate the break-even rate required per shoot day, to recover equipment costs only, listing the equipment, quantity, realistic purchase rate and the repayment period required. This empowers you to know what your equipment actually costs you and helps you to motivate the charging of Digital Capture Fees.

The cost of insuring the equipment is then added to this to determine the minimum DCF you need to recoup per shoot day. The basic formula used is based on 11 working months per year, allowing for 15 days annual leave and 5 days sick leave per year, and 10 actual shoot days per month with a working month based on 20.75 days. Considering that every shoot requires pre and post production 10 shoot days is a reasonable target.

BASIC EQUIPMENT COSTING

No	Description	Unit	Qty	Rate	Total	RP	Total per year
1	Canon EOS 5d Mk3	Ea	2	38,995.00	77,990.00	3	25,996.67
2	Canon EF 24-70mm F2.8 LII USM Lens	Ea	1	27,995.00	27,995.00	5	5,599.00
3	Canon EF 70-200mm F2.8 LII USM Lens	Ea	1	31,995.00	31,995.00	5	6,399.00
4	Canon 600 EX-RT Speed-light Flash	Ea	2	9,395.00	18,790.00	5	3,758.00
5	Manfrotto Tripod Kit with 3way head	Ea	1	5,195.00	5,195.00	5	1,039.00
6	Lowepro Fastpack 350 Backpack Camera Bag	Ea	1	2,495.00	2,495.00	5	499.00
7	Flash Meter Sekonic L-478D	Ea	1	8,695.00	8,695.00	5	1,739.00
8	Matin 103cm Collapsible Reflector Kit 5 in 1	Ea	1	695.00	695.00	3	231.67
9	Gary Fong Light-sphere	Ea	1	1,095.00	1,095.00	3	365.00
10	Memory Card 16GB Sandisk SD	Ea	8	830.00	6,640.00	1	6,640.00
11	Battery Grip Booster Pack Canon BG E11	Ea	2	7,005.00	14,010.00	3	4,670.00
12	Spare Batteries Canon LP-E6	Ea	6	1,485.00	8,910.00	3	2,970.00
13	Hahnel TC Novo Synergy Rechargeable AA	Ea	4	250.00	1,000.00	1	1,000.00
14	Filter Set	Set	1	2,500.00	2,500.00	3	833.33
15	Cleaning Kit Digital Deluxe	Ea	1	150.00	150.00	1	150.00
16	External Hard Drive 1TB	Ea	4	2,495.00	9,980.00	1	9,980.00

17	Macbook Pro 15-inch Retina Q-Core i7 2.5G/16Gb/512 Flash	Ea	1	46,299.00	46,299.00	3	15,433.00
18	Adobe CC Photographer	Mnth	12	145.00	1,740.00	1	1,740.00

Subtotal	**266,174.00**	**89,042.67**
Break-even rate per month based on *11 months per year*		8,094.79
Digital Equipment Insurance / month		1,618.96
Allowance for repairs & maintenance @ 10%		809.48
Depreciation (straight line, 3years, recovered in 11 months PA)		8,065.88
Finance Costs, interest rate @11%, recovered in 11 months PA		890.43
Break-even rate per shoot day based on *10 shoot days per month*		1,947.95
Profit markup @ 25%		486.99
DCF MINIMUM RATE / DAY - EXCLUDING PROCESSING TIME		**2,434.94**

RP = Repayment/Replacement Period (in years)

Please note that the above rates per item were taken from a South African online camera equipment retailer and were correct at the time of writing. The prices fluctuate with time and the R/$ exchange rate.

As can be seen from the above table you need to recover **R 2 434.94** per day from your DCF to pay off and maintain your basic equipment, EXCLUDING PROCESSING TIME.

There are currently two main methods of charging DCFs in the industry, with an alternative Post Production Fee.

METHOD 1

The following digital capture fee method is for images captured with a digital SLR - **NOT medium format digital**. Medium format digital camera equipment is approximately three times the price of DSLR and the rate should therefore be tripled.

Method 1 is the method currently used by some magazines and advertising agencies.

The rate is per final image supplied (digitally processed, un-retouched), according to the client's shot list. Please note that standard industry practice is to supply ONE final image per shot required by the client and as such the DCF is based on the number of final images supplied, according to the client's shot list.

The following DCFs, charged per image according to the shot list, are based on generally accepted industry standards for DSLR Cameras:

SUBJECT	Ea
FASHION	285.00
PORTRAITURE	175.00
PRODUCTS	125.00

The flaw in this system is that a photographer is often commissioned to shoot a portrait, for example, in a half day. Even if the photographer does two half day portrait shoots in a day the DCFs for the day will be R 330.00 that means that the photographer will under recover on his/her equipment by

R 2 434.94 - R 330.00 = R 2 104.94

The loss will have to be covered from the photographer's fee. Considering that the photographer needs to charge **R11 492.14** as a day rate (based on the day rate calculation) and **R 2 434.94** for DCFs totalling **R13 927.08** for the day, if doing two half day shoots for a magazine at their specified (take it or leave it) rates:

2 x R1 750.00 Half day editorial fee	3,500.00
2 x R175.00 Portrait DCF	350.00
	3,850.00
Less recovery required	-13,927.08
LOSS for the day	**-10,077.08**

The photographer is paying the magazine R10 077.08 for a byline that is in truth his/her legal moral right, if asserted, without being paid for processing time. Clearly this is not sustainable business practice.

METHOD 2

Digital capture fee method for images captured with a digital SLR - NOT medium format digital. Medium format digital camera equipment is approximately three times the price of DSLR and the rate should therefore be tripled.

The rate is per final image supplied (digitally processed, un-retouched). Method 2 is more financially viable and sustainable for the photographer and includes processing time.

No. Final Images Supplied	Ea
1 - 10 images (minimum fee)	2,450.00
11 - 15 (per image supplied)	232.75
16 - 20 (per image supplied)	221.00
21+ (per image supplied)	210.00

METHOD 3 - POST PRODUCTION FEE

The third method is simply charging for post production on an hourly basis at a rate per hour. This is not a Digital Capture Fee but rather a Post Production Fee, that should be costed up front and recorded in the Cost Estimate. It is an estimate of the number of hours required for selecting and processing out the final images in preparation for retouching, charged accordingly.

RETOUCHING FEE

There seems to be gross misunderstanding in the industry between editing and retouching. Many people refer to editing when they mean retouching.

Editing is the process of downloading the images to the computer, selecting the final images, making basic corrections to those images such as exposure, white balance, contrast, vibrance and saturation and entering the meta data. Image editing software such as Adobe Lightroom, Adobe Bridge, Apple's Aperture or Phase One's Capture One is used for editing.

Once the image is exported from the image editing software and opened in Adobe Photoshop the process then becomes retouching. Retouching is a specialised function and is not included in a photographer's standard scope of work. Whilst there are some photographers who are technically skilled enough to retouch their own images, most are not. Just as in the past photographers would hand over their processed film for scanning and retouching, so should they now hand over their processed digital images for retouching to a specialist repro trained retoucher.

The retouching fee covers the repro retoucher's time, equipment and other overheads.

Retouching should only be done by operators qualified to do so. Photographers should not retouch their own work unless they are repro trained and are qualified to do so, however photographers should oversee the retouching process in order to ensure that the final image to be used fulfils their creative vision and standards.

Professional retouchers currently charge between R300-R500/hour in South Africa, depending on their level of expertise. Skilled, experienced retouchers can do more in an hour than less skilled operators and often work out more cost effective in total, despite their higher rate per hour. If the photographer outsources the retouching then the standard profit margin should be added before being billed to the client.

RATES FOR CDs, DVDs, UPLOADS

The rates to supply and burn disks, to upload to a FTP server and to archive images cover the material supply, use of the equipment (hardware and software), the operator's time, related costs and other overheads. These costs should be calculated for your own business yourself, however, current industry averages are:

TYPE	Ea
Supply & Burn CD	200.00
Supply & Burn DVD	310.00
Upload to FTP Server / Mb	2.50
Digital Archiving / Mb	3.75

Digital Archiving is the storage, and backing up of the storage, of all the shots and related files from a photo shoot. This includes the camera raw files as well as the corrected, processed out and retouched images. Whilst certain shoots can be stored on DVDs it is advisable to store archives on external hard drives as well. Whatever storage method you choose you should always have a backup of the archive. A backup means that you have a second, duplicate copy of the original files on another storage source. Backups are essential in today's digital age to ensure that data is not lost permanently if a storage system fails, is lost, damaged or stolen. This does however mean that the archive storage method cost is essentially doubled. The rate above considers this and is to archive and backup on external hard drives.

Some clients may tell you that you don't need to archive their work as they will do it. This is not recommended as first you should not hand over your camera raw files to your client and second if their archive fails, they will come back to you for the images if they need them again. Archiving is good professional practice.

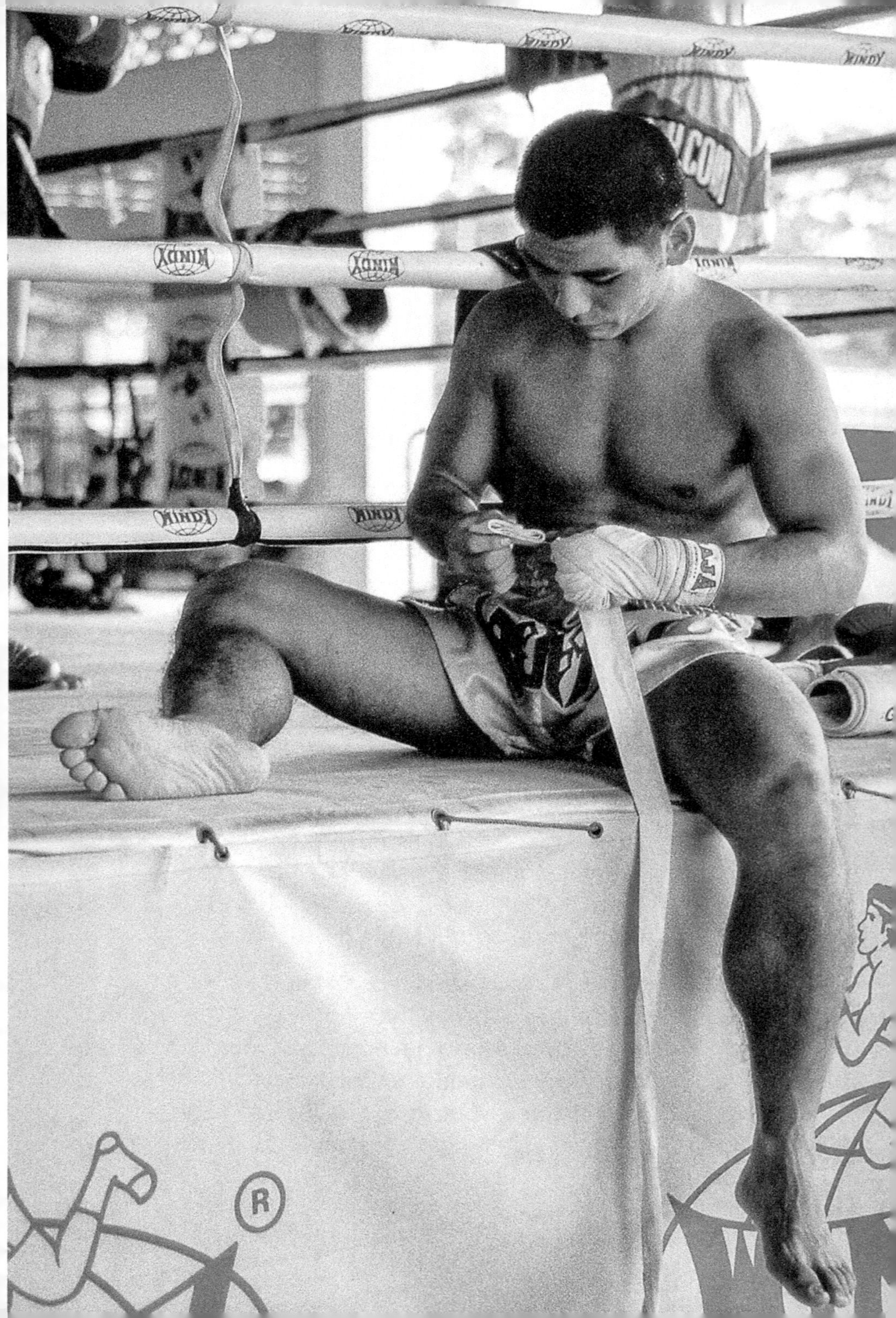
WINDY

CHAPTER 11

INTERPRETING A BRIEF

"Photography's like this baby that needs to be fed all the time. It's always hungry. It needs to be read to, taken care of."

Annie Leibovitz

The brief is one of the most important documents in professional photography. The brief is a written description of a client's photography requirements for a particular assignment, usually compiled and issued by the client's advertising agency, or in the case of editorial by the art director or picture editor. The brief forms the base document that is used by the photographer to compile their cost estimate for the job and it is essential for the brief to be informative, descriptive, clear and concise.

When receiving a brief for the preparation of a cost estimate for a photographic shoot, the brief needs to answer 5 main questions:

1. **WHO** - Exactly who is commissioning you and what are their official contact details including physical address, postal address, telephone number, mobile telephone number, fax number and email address. Ensure that the address details on the cost estimate are the same as the details required for the invoice.
2. **WHAT** - Exactly what do they need you to shoot and for what usage?
3. **WHERE** - Where do they want to shoot. What are the implications of the locations?
4. **WHEN** - When are the proposed shoot dates. Has provision been made for weather days?
5. **HOW** - Do they specify how they want the scene/subject shot? Are there any visual references?

Ensure that you refer back to these five questions whilst preparing your cost estimate and that you cover the expenses related to them in your cost estimate. A thoroughly prepared cost estimate will help you to uncover hidden costs and save you nasty surprises during production.

There is something referred to in the industry as the 'Professional Under-brief'. This is a technique used by unethical people in which they provide the photographer with an intentionally vague brief with the intention of ensuring that the photographer overcommits to a shoot, to the commissioning agent's financial benefit. The photographer is forced to absorb costs that he or she did not consider when costing the job due to the vague nature of the brief.

By repeatedly asking yourself these five questions while preparing a cost estimate you can reduce the chance of this happening. No matter how urgently the commissioning agent needs your cost estimate, always make the time to ask for details if the brief is not clear.

Ensure that your Cost Estimate for the brief is dated and has a validity period, for example, "This Cost Estimate is valid for 30 days." Costs in the photographic industry vary according to a number of factors, the main two being the foreign exchange rate and inflation. Jobs are sometimes delayed for various reasons and you may need to re-cost a job should it be delayed, especially if it rolls over into a new financial year.

It is essential to clarify who will be responsible for the payment of travel and subsistence costs as well. They should either be included or excluded in your estimate, depending on the brief's requirements.

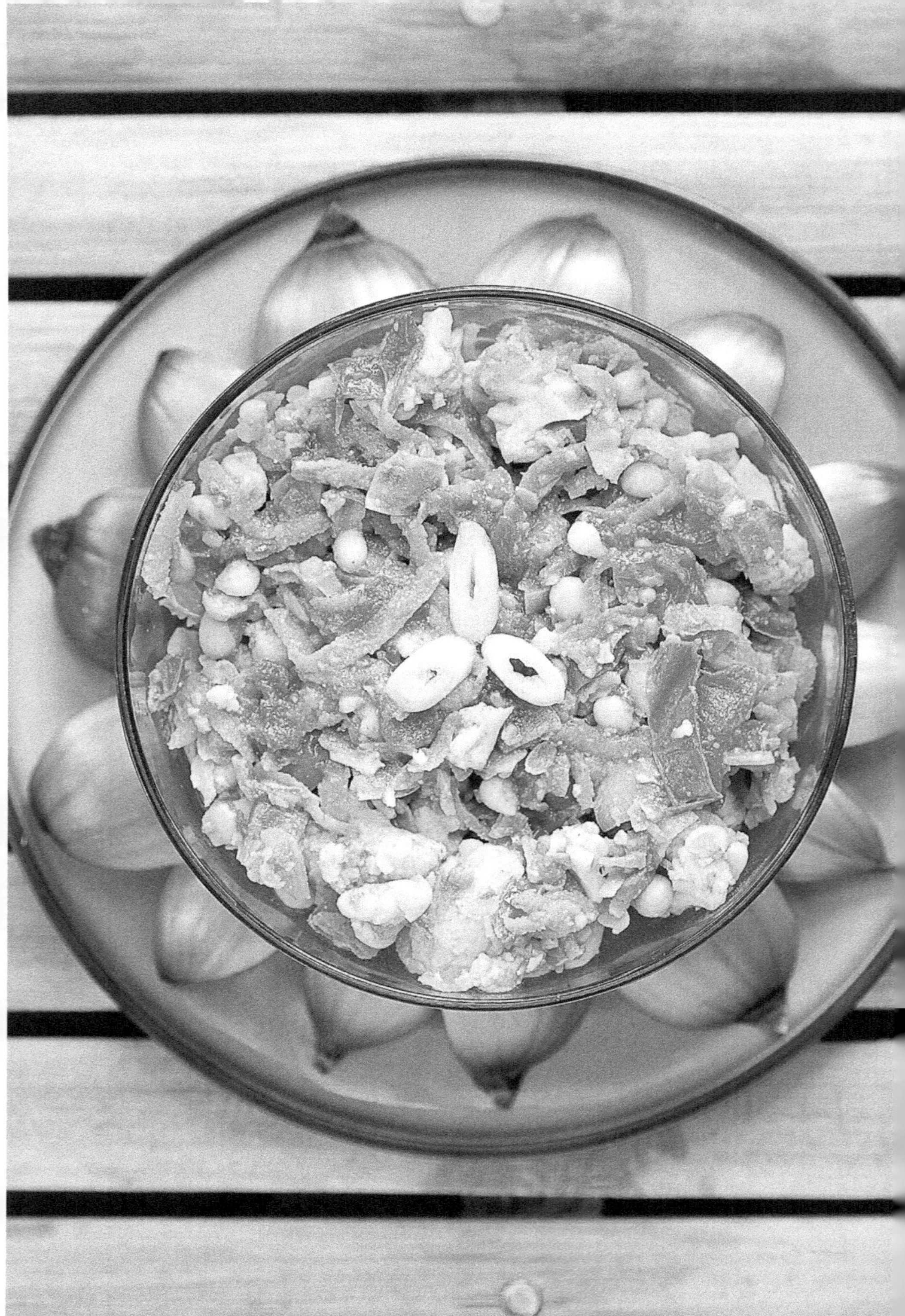

CHAPTER 12

ESSENTIAL PAPERWORK

"You've got to push yourself harder. You've got to start looking for pictures nobody else could take. You've got to take the tools you have and probe deeper."

William Albert Allard

The use of paperwork to clarify business agreements is standard to all businesses. Photography is no exception. Some of the information photographers need to clarify with their clients is:

1. The **scope of work** to be performed in the form of a written brief with visual references. This should come from the client.
2. The **financial value** of the work to be performed in the form of a cost estimate.
3. **Copyright ownership**
4. **License for Use** clearly stating the permitted TIME, TERRITORY AND MEDIA.
5. **Reuse terms**
6. **Terms of payment**
7. Terms for the resolution of the **breach** of the agreement.

TERMS & CONDITIONS

All photographers should use terms and conditions either on, or attached to their cost estimates. The terms and conditions should clarify the terms on which you are accepting the commission including your payment terms, copyright ownership, ownership of materials, indemnity and right to a credit to name but a few. Your terms and conditions must be submitted at the cost estimate stage to form part of the job contract documentation. Submitting them on your invoice is post fact and is not legally binding. You can however also record your terms and conditions on your invoice to reinforce them.

It is important to specify a 'No Archive' term on your cost estimate, especially for editorial clients. This means that once the client has used the image, they may not store or archive the image in any form, and must delete it. The reason for this is that staff members change and an outgoing staff member is unlikely to inform an incoming staff member of all the licenses to use images in their archives.

COST ESTIMATE

A cost estimate is what the name implies, an estimate of cost. A cost estimate is a variable document and can change according to a number of factors. This is essential to photography as there are so many external influences beyond a photographers control that can influence a shoot, like the weather. Even if asked to submit a quotation a photographer should always title the document a 'cost estimate'.

Your cost estimate is probably the most important piece of paperwork surrounding a job as it forms the base contract for that job. It signifies your acceptance of the offer of a commission and details your understanding of the job, the approximate cost and your terms and conditions. Always send a cost estimate, even if you are 'donating' your time or skill as jobs that you shoot for free need a written base agreement.

The layout of a cost estimate is flexible and you should develop one that suits you and your business. Information essential to a cost estimate regardless of the layout is:

1. The heading 'Cost Estimate'.

2. The date of the cost estimate.
3. The client's (commissioning agent's) full name, registered name of their business, VAT number, physical address, telephone number, fax number and e mail address. This will transfer to the invoice.
4. Your Base Usage Rate (BUR) for the shoot with your License for Use specifications.
5. The amount you are prepared to execute the job for, including VAT. VAT should be shown separately to the subtotal if you are VAT registered.
6. Your terms and conditions.
7. Your cost estimate should either be on your letterhead, that contains the registered name of your business, your VAT number, physical address, telephone number, fax number and e mail address, or the layout should be customised to clearly display this information.

A commonly used layout of a cost estimate is the 'itemised' layout. Each line item of the estimate is listed with an item number, description of that item, unit of measurement, quantity required, rate per unit and the total for that line item. The advantage of itemised cost estimates is that they assist you to think carefully about everything you need to fulfil the brief requirements for the production of the photo shoot. An efficient way of working with itemised estimates is to develop a template using spreadsheet software like Microsoft Excel or Apple's Numbers. The same template can be used for estimating all jobs with line items added or deleted as required for that job. The itemised cost estimate layout works well for larger productions. Smaller productions such as social shoots require much simpler cost estimates.

YOUR BUSINESS LETTERHEAD HERE

COST ESTIMATE

Invoice Address	Client	ABC Fashion
ABC Fashion House (Pty) Ltd	Client rep	Ms. F. Garment
VAT No. 555 XXX 12345	Shoot name	SS16
136 Mansel Drive	Shoot rep	Ms. S. Creatif
Killarney	Shoot dates	14-15 Sep 2016
Gauteng	Job no.	13/104
Tel 011 555 4242	Payment	**COD**
garment@abcfashion.co.za	Date	12 June 2016

Item	Description	Unit	Qty	Rate	Total
	PHOTOGRAPHER'S FEE				
1	Photographic Charge BUR Catalogue & Social Media	Day	2	15,000.00	30,000.00
2	Pre & post production meetings, briefing & castings	Hr	5	1,250.00	6,250.00
3	Location scouting and light checks	Hr	8	1,250.00	10,000.00
	PRODUCTION EXPENSES				
4	Photographic assistant	%	15	30,000.00	4,500.00
5	Consumables	P/sum	1	500.00	500.00
6	Lighting - Portable strobe lighting	Day	1	2,500.00	2,500.00
7	Additional lighting - Scrims/ Diffusors/Reflectors	Day	1	1,350.00	1,350.00
8	Accessories	P/Sum	1	850.00	850.00
9	Studio hire	Day	1	3,500.00	3,500.00
10	Studio consumables	Sum	1	500.00	500.00
11	Mileage	Km	34	3.24	110.16
12	Hair and make up Artist	Day	1	3,500.00	3,500.00
13	Assistant Fashion Stylist - pre production and returns	Day	1	3,375.00	3,375.00

14	Assistant Fashion Stylist - Shoot (on set)	Day	1	4,500.00	4,500.00
15	Clothing and props Hire	P/sum	1	7,500.00	7,500.00
16	Models - (Online Catalogue (RSA) & Social Media 1 year)	Day	3	12,500.00	37,500.00
17	Location - Permits	Ea	1	1,500.00	1,500.00
18	Location - Private 1	Day	1	10,000.00	10,000.00
19	Catering - On set CRAFT & LUNCH (Full day)	Ea	16	175.00	2,800.00
20	Catering - On set CRAFT only (Half day)	Ea	0	95.00	0.00
21	Digital Capture Fee - Fashion	Ea	24	265.00	6,360.00
22	Retouching (outsourced)	Hr	50	456.00	22,800.00
23	Supply of image CD	Ea	0	165.00	0.00
24	Supply of image DVD	Ea	1	265.00	265.00
25	Upload to FTP server	Mb	300	0.75	225.00
26	Archiving - Backup of images on external hard drive	Gb	30.24	3.00	90.72
27	Courier to client - Overnight Express	P/Sum	1	365.00	365.00

Total incl. VAT (Non VAT Vendor) **R 160,840.88**

1 This Cost Estimate is valid for 30 days from date.

2 Please note my standard terms and conditions applicable to all shoots at http://www.[yourwebsite]/standard-terms-conditions/

3 The commencement of the shoot signifies the acceptance of the standard terms and conditions in full.

WEDDINGS / SOCIAL PHOTOGRAPHY

Cost estimates and invoices for wedding or social photography are much simpler. Most wedding/social photographers offer different packages at different rates. The cost estimate needs to fulfil all the requirements but instead of itemising everything can simply list the agreed on package, like the following example.

YOUR BUSINESS LETTERHEAD HERE

COST ESTIMATE

Invoice Address	Client	Mrs. Brides Mother
Mrs. Brides Mother	Client rep	Mrs. Brides Mother
123 Lovers Lane	Shoot name	Wedding Amore
Claremont	Shoot rep	Mrs. Brides Mother
Cape Town	Shoot dates	17 September 2016
Tel 021 555 4242	Job no.	13/104
Fax 021 555 4243	Payment terms	**70% deposit, bal COD**
bmother@gmail.com	Date	12 June 2016

Item	Description		Total
1	**WEDDING PACKAGE 1** (140 Hi Res Images on disk, maximum 9 hrs, overtime charged at R2 085,00/hr or part thereof)		15,000.00
2	**COFFEE TABLE BOOK** (40 pages)		5,000.00
	Total incl. VAT (Non VAT Vendor)	**R**	**20,000.00**

1 This Cost Estimate is valid for 30 days from date.

2 Please note my standard terms and conditions applicable to all shoots at http://www.[yourwebsite]/standard-terms-conditions/

3 The commencement of the shoot signifies the acceptance of the standard terms and conditions in full.

A less intimidating method of recording terms and conditions is to create a 'Standard Terms and Conditions' page on your web site that you refer to in your Cost Estimate, instead of listing your terms and conditions in full on your cost estimates. An example of this is:

"Please note my standard terms and conditions applicable to all shoots at http://www.deryckvs.com/standard-terms-conditions/"

By doing this you are fulfilling the legal requirement of drawing your clients attention to your terms and conditions and informing them of where they can find them to read them.

There is no set formula or one right way for drawing up cost estimates or invoices. Whilst the basic principles should be adhered to you can and should be creative in the way you present yours. After all photography is a creative field.

TERMS AND CONDITIONS

The following terms and conditions were drawn up in conjunction with an Attorney who is satisfied they are legally sound and binding. You are welcome to copy them for use as your standard terms and conditions for inclusion either directly on your cost estimates or on your website page referred to in your cost estimates.

Standard Terms and Conditions

Please note the following standard terms and conditions that form part of all cost estimates applicable to all commissioned shoots.

1. *It is hereby agreed that the Photographer is recognised and constituted as the Author of the commissioned works produced and shall be the owner of the copyright therein throughout the world . A License to Use is granted to the Client for the specified use. No other right besides those specifically included in the license are granted in respect of the work(s).*

2. *This License is conditioned upon receipt of payment in full by the Photographer within the payment period agreed. All rights not expressly granted to the Client remain the exclusive property of the Photographer. The Client may not transfer or assign this License without the express written consent of the Photographer. "Client" refers to the person or organisation, its representatives, successors, assignees, agents and affiliates requesting the provision of photographic services and supply of photographs.*

3. *Images commissioned for the shoot require approval by the Client on set. Should images be rejected for any reason whatsoever after the shoot the Client will be liable for the payment of the Invoice based on the final Cost Estimate in full. No license as contemplated in clause 1 is granted in respect of rejected images notwithstanding payment as aforementioned*

4. *Where additional expenses are incurred by the Photographer due to changes in the original brief by the Client or by circumstances beyond the Photographer's control, the Client agrees to*

pay such reasonable expenses and/or fees at the Photographer's normal rates.

5. *The commencement of the shoot signifies the acceptance of the final Cost Estimate in it's entirety and the adoption of this agreement by the parties. This Agreement constitutes the sole record of the agreement between the parties and supersedes all previous agreements.*
6. *For editorial use, the Client agrees to provide a credit line in the form of the Photographer's trading name in type no smaller than the nearest text and immediately adjacent to the picture used or the editorial fee is converted to the full commercial fee.*
7. *The Client agrees to indemnify and save harmless the Photographer against all liabilities, claims and legal costs arising out of the Client's use of the photographs.*
8. *The Photographer retains the right to use the Photographs in any manner, at any time and in any part of the world for self promotional purposes.*
9. *In the event of non-payment or other breach of this agreement by the Client, the Client shall pay all of the Photographers costs and expenses incurred in the enforcement of the terms of this agreement, including the Photographer's attorney's fees and the license contemplated in clause 1 shall not exist and be of no force or effect.*

10. *No variation of the terms of this contract shall be recognised unless agreed in writing.*
11. *This agreement shall be governed by the laws of the Republic of South Africa.*
12. *Interest at 2.5% per month will be charged on all overdue accounts.*

INVOICE

Your invoice can follow the same format as your cost estimate with final figures on it. You can record your terms and conditions on your invoice as well.

Information essential to an invoice regardless of the layout is:

1. The heading 'Tax Invoice'.
2. The date of the invoice.
3. Your VAT number or if not VAT registered the words *"Non VAT Vendor"* or *"Not VAT Registered"*.
4. The client's (commissioning agent's) full name, registered name of their business, VAT number, physical address, telephone number, fax number and e mail address.
5. A clear description of the products or services you are selling.
6. Payment terms.
7. Your banking details if payment is required by EFT (Electronic Funds Transfer).
8. Your invoice should either be on your letterhead that contains the registered name of your

business, your VAT number, physical address, telephone number, fax number and e mail address or the layout should be customised to clearly display this information.

9. A footnote thanking your clients for their business, clarifying where the proof of payment should be sent (fax/e mail).

YOUR BUSINESS LETTERHEAD HERE

TAX INVOICE

VAT No. 555 XXX 12345

Invoice Address	Client	ABC Fashion
ABC Fashion House (Pty) Ltd	Client rep	Ms. F. Garment
VAT No. 555 XXX 12345	Shoot name	SS13
136 Mansel Drive	Shoot rep	Ms. S. Creatif
Killarney	Shoot dates	14-15 Sep 2016
Gauteng	Job no.	13/104
Tel 011 555 4242	Payment	**COD**
fgarment@abcfashion.co.za	Date	16/09/2016

Item	Description	Unit	Qty	Rate	Total
	PHOTOGRAPHER'S FEE				
1	Photographic Charge BUR Catalogue & Social Media	Day	2	15,000.00	30,000.00
2	Pre & post production meetings, briefing & castings	Hr	5	1,250.00	6,250.00
3	Location scouting and light checks	Hr	8	1,250.00	10,000.00
	PRODUCTION EXPENSES				
4	Photographic assistant	%	15	30,000.00	4,500.00
5	Consumables	P/sum	1	500.00	500.00
6	Lighting - Portable strobe lighting	Day	1	2,500.00	2,500.00
7	Additional lighting - Scrims/Diffusors/ Reflectors	Day	1	1,350.00	1,350.00
8	Accessories	P/Sum	1	850.00	850.00
9	Studio hire	Day	1	3,500.00	3,500.00
10	Studio consumables	Sum	1	500.00	500.00
11	Mileage	Km	34	3.24	110.16
12	Hair and make up Artist	Day	1	3,500.00	3,500.00

13	Assistant Fashion Stylist - pre production and returns	Day	1	3,375.00	3,375.00
14	Assistant Fashion Stylist - Shoot (on set)	Day	1	4,500.00	4,500.00
15	Clothing and props Hire	P/sum	1	7,500.00	7,500.00
16	Models - (Online Catalogue (RSA) & Social Media 1 year)	Day	3	12,500.00	37,500.00
17	Location - Permits	Ea	1	1,500.00	1,500.00
18	Location - Private 1	Day	1	10,000.00	10,000.00
19	Catering - On set CRAFT & LUNCH (Full day)	Ea	16	175.00	2,800.00
20	Catering - On set CRAFT only (Half day)	Ea	0	95.00	0.00
21	Digital Capture Fee - Fashion	Ea	24	265.00	6,360.00
22	Retouching (outsourced)	Hr	50	456.00	22,800.00
23	Supply of image CD	Ea	0	165.00	0.00
24	Supply of image DVD	Ea	1	265.00	265.00
25	Upload to FTP server	Mb	300	0.75	225.00
26	Archiving - Backup of images on external hard drive	Gb	30.24	3.00	90.72
27	Courier to client - Overnight Express	P/Sum	1	365.00	365.00

Total incl. VAT (Non VAT Vendor) **R 160,840.88**

1 An Exclusive License for Use is granted to the Client for South Africa, for Catalogue and Social Media use, in perpetuity. No other right besides those specifically included in the license are granted in respect of the work(s).

2 This License for Use transfers on receipt of full and final payment.

3 Please make payment into Cheque Account Number 1234 5678 910, held at XXX Bank, Branch Code 123 456, held in the name of *photographers business name*.

4 Interest of 2,5% per month will be charged on overdue accounts.

5 No Archive. The image(s) may not be stored or archived after insertion and must be deleted.

Unfortunately not all clients pay their bills when they are due resulting in cash flow problems for you. If your payment terms have been clearly communicated on your invoice, you have sent a statement of account, and your client still does not pay then you need to consider taking further action. Your book keeper can send a standard, politely but firmly worded letter to your client, asking them to settle the outstanding amount, in full, by a specified date, followed up by a phone call to ensure that they have received the letter. If they do not make payment in full by the specified date you may need to hand them over to a debt collection agency to collect the outstanding money on your behalf. There are many debt collection agencies who work on a commission only basis, in other words, they charge commission on the amount that they successfully collect, with no further charges to you. Remember that should you hand a client over for debt collection they are unlikely to book you again in future however, no business is better than bad business as it costs you less.

LICENSE FOR USE

The license for use should be recorded on both your cost estimate and your invoice and should give a clear view of what both you and the client may do with the image(s).

A license for use is based on three factors:

1. TIME, measured in years.
2. TERRITORY, being countries or groups of countries defined by borders.

3. MEDIA, being specific types of media like billboard, point of sale and magazines.

The license for use must include the allowable media, time period and territory, as well as whether it is an exclusive or non-exclusive license for use. A standard license for use usually includes two media, for one year, in one territory OR one media, for two years, in one territory. The time and media are interchangeable, the territories are not.

The licence begins on first insertion and first insertion can be expected within 6 months of the delivery of the finished job to the agency/client. It is recommended that work be licensed for a minimum period of 6 months. Less than 6 months in an advertising context is unrealistic.

An editorial license for use is once off use, in one edition of the publication only.

EXCLUSIVE/NON-EXCLUSIVE

The industry standard in advertising is exclusive license for use, normally for a minimum of 6 months. This reassures the client that the images they have commissioned will not be used by anyone else, anywhere else, sabotaging their campaign.

Editorial exclusivity is normally three months from the time of first insertion.

Once the initial exclusivity period has expired, the client should be offered first choice to renew it. Should they decide not to, then the images can be used for other purposes.

In advertising it is recommended that commissioned images not be used for any other purpose, other than self promotional purposes by the photographer, unless both client and agency permission is obtained, for four years from the expiration date of the license. This is to avoid use of the images by competitor or undesirable brands.

The photographer should always reserve the right to use the images for self promotional purposes (PR), from the time of first insertion. This means that once the images have been published the photographer may use them in his/her portfolio, web site, composite cards, portfolio web sites and competition entries, as well as other marketing materials, to promote his/her talent and expertise. Crediting the people and agencies involved in the use of the images is fair practice.

A non-exclusive license for use means that the images may be bought and used by other parties during the same time period. Non-exclusive licenses for use are not common, but are sometimes agreed to when agreeing to low budget jobs so that the photographer has a chance to increase their income from other peoples use of the images.

RE-USAGE GUIDELINES

The license for use and reuse guidelines are widely used as a negotiating point throughout the world and have been adopted and adapted by countries in Europe, the USA, South Africa and Australia. The BUR, as stated on the estimate and invoice, is the figure that these re-usage guideline percentages are based on. The

Association of Photographers (AOP), a London based international professional photographers association, has done an incredible amount of work on reuse of photographs. They have a usage calculator on their web site that is user friendly and easy to understand should you need assistance with calculating usage value.[7] The usage value is the combined value of the time period required, the number of media the images will be used in and the territories in which the images will be used.

MODEL/PROPERTY RELEASE FORMS

A model release form, or release form, is simply a contract between a photographer and a model in which a model gives his/her consent for images of themselves to be used in a particular way. Considering that models are paid according to time, territory and media it is essential for a model release to contain this information. Releases should be used for all shoots with people in them, whether they are professional models or not, and copies of the releases given to the model and the client for their record purposes. Minors may not sign model releases, the release must be signed by their parent or guardian. In South Africa a minor is anyone under the age of eighteen years old.

It's a good idea to attach a picture of the model to the model release for ease of identification at a later stage.

There are many model and property releases available from associations like the Association of

[7] http://www.the-aop.org/information/usage-calculator

Photographers (www.the-aop.org), the American Society of Media Photographers (www.asmp.com) and from photo libraries like Gallo Images (www.galloimages.com). You can either use these as they are or adapt them for your business. Considering that literacy is an issue in South Africa, it helps if the wording of the model/property release is as simple as possible whilst remaining legally binding.

The allowed use should be included in both the cost estimate and the final invoice to client so that there is no misunderstanding later. If the client wants to use the images for extended use, then they may have to pay both the photographer and the model for the rights to do so. Normally the type of use is the same for both the model and the photographer.

Most photo/stock libraries require both model and property releases in order for images to be sold through the photo library. It can be quite difficult to track down people you have photographed in the past for them to sign model releases, which is why it's best to do it on set at the time of the shoot.

A property release form is similar to a model release but is a contract between the property owner and photographer in which the property owner, or their appointed representative, agrees to the use of the property in the images. A tenant of the property normally does not have the authority to sign a property release, it must be signed by the owner or their representative.

ADULT MODEL/PERFORMER AGREEMENT RELEASE

Release #: ______________________________

Date/s of production/s: ______________________

Model: ______________________________

Address: ______________________________

____

Phone No: ______________________________

Model's Age (at time of production): ______________

Model's Ethnicity (optional): ________________

Description of production/s: ________________

____

____

____

Place photo of model in box.

THIS MODEL AGREEMENT AND RELEASE ("Agreement") is dated __________ and is between the undersigned photographer ("Photographer") and the undersigned model/performer ("I"). Agreement as follows:

For good and valuable consideration of ______________________________ I hereby grant the undersigned Photographer permission to photograph me. I further give my irrevocable consent to Photographer and his/her direct or indirect licensees and assignees to publish, republish or otherwise transmit the images of myself in any medium for all purposes throughout the world. I understand that the images may be altered or modified in any manner. I hereby waive any right that I may have to inspect and approve a finished product or the copy that may be used in connection with an image that the Photographer has taken of me, or the use to which it may be applied. I further release the Photographer and his/her direct or indirect licensees and assignees, from any claims for remuneration
Associated with any form of damage, foreseen or unforseen, associated with the use of the images.

I am of legal age and have the full legal capacity to execute this authorization without the consent or knowledge of any other person.

AGREED BY THE MODEL/PERFORMER	PHOTOGRAPHER
______________________________ Signature	______________________________ Signature
Print Name: ______________________	Print Name: ______________________
Date: ______________________	Address: ______________________

MINOR MODEL/PERFORMER RELEASE AGREEMENT

Release #: ______________________________

Date/s of production/s: ______________________________

Photographer name: ______________________________

Model: ______________________________

Address: ______________________________

____

Phone No: ______________________________

Model's Age (at time of production): ______________

Model's Ethnicity: ______________________

Description of production/s: ______________________

____

Place photo of model in box.

In consideration of the engagement as a model of the minor named above, and for other good and valuable consideration of__________________________ herein acknowledged as received, upon the terms hereinafter stated, I hereby grant to______________________ ("Photographer"), his/her legal representatives and assigns, those for whom Photographer is acting, and those acting with his/her authority and permission, the absolute right and permission to take, use, reuse, publish, and republish photographic portraits or pictures of the minor or in which the minor may be included, in whole or in part, or composite or distorted in character or form, without restriction as to changes or alterations from time to time, in conjunction with the minor's own or a fictitious name, or reproductions thereof in color or otherwise, made through any medium at his/her studios or elsewhere, and in any and all media now or hereafter known, for art, advertising, trade, or any other purpose whatsoever. I also consent to the use of any published matter in conjunction therewith.

I hereby waive any right that I or the minor may have to inspect or approve the finished product or products or the advertising copy or printed matter that may be used in connection therewith or the use to which it may be applied.

I hereby release, discharge, and agree to save harmless and defend Photographer, his/her legal representatives or assigns, and all persons acting under his/her permission or authority or those for whom he/she is acting, from any liability by virtue of any blurring, distortion, alteration, optical illusion, or use in composite form, whether intentional or otherwise, that may occur or be produced in the taking of said picture or in any subsequent processing thereof, as well as any publication thereof, including without limitation any claims for libel or violation of any right of publicity or privacy.

I hereby warrant that I am of full age and have every right to contract for the minor in the above regard. I state further that I have read the above authorization, release, and agreement, prior to its execution, and that I am fully familiar with the contents thereof. This release shall be binding upon the minor and me, and our respective heirs, legal representatives, and assigns.

Parent or Guardian's Signature______________________________

Parent/Guardian Name______________________________

Email address______________________________

Parent or Guardian phone (if differs from minor)______________

Witness Signature______________________________

Witness Name(print) :______________________________

PROPERTY/ LOCATION RELEASE

This Property/Location Agreement and Release ("Agreement") is dated ______________

And is between ____________________________("photographer") and the undersigned

Property Owner. Agreement as follows:

For good and valuable consideration of ___________________, herein acknowledged as received, the undersigned ("Property Owner") being the legal owner of and/or have the authority to bind the owner of, or having the right to permit the taking and use of, the photographs of certain property identified as :

Place: ____

agrees that the photographs of the property identified above may be supplied by the photographer or his or her licensees or assigns to any person for any use whatsoever, whole or in part, in any manner, without seeking further permission or consideration.

The undersigned hereby waives all rights and releases Photographer and its assigns from, and shall neither sue nor bring any proceeding against any such parties for, any liability, loss, demands, claims or causes of action, whether now known or unknown, for trademark or any similar matter, or based upon or relating to the use and exploitation of the images of the Property.

Copyright in the photographs does not belong to undersigned or any other person photographed or, if the photographs were commissioned by undersigned, such copyright is hereby assigned to the Photographer.

Executed as of the date first written above.

Individual Owners

____
Owners Name(Please Print)

____
Owners Signature

____
Date Phone Number

Photographer

____
(Print Name)

____
Signature

____
Date

Corporate Ownership

____
Employees Name (Please Print)

____
Employees Signature

____
Position/Title

____
Name of Corporation

____
Address

____
Phone Number

____
Date

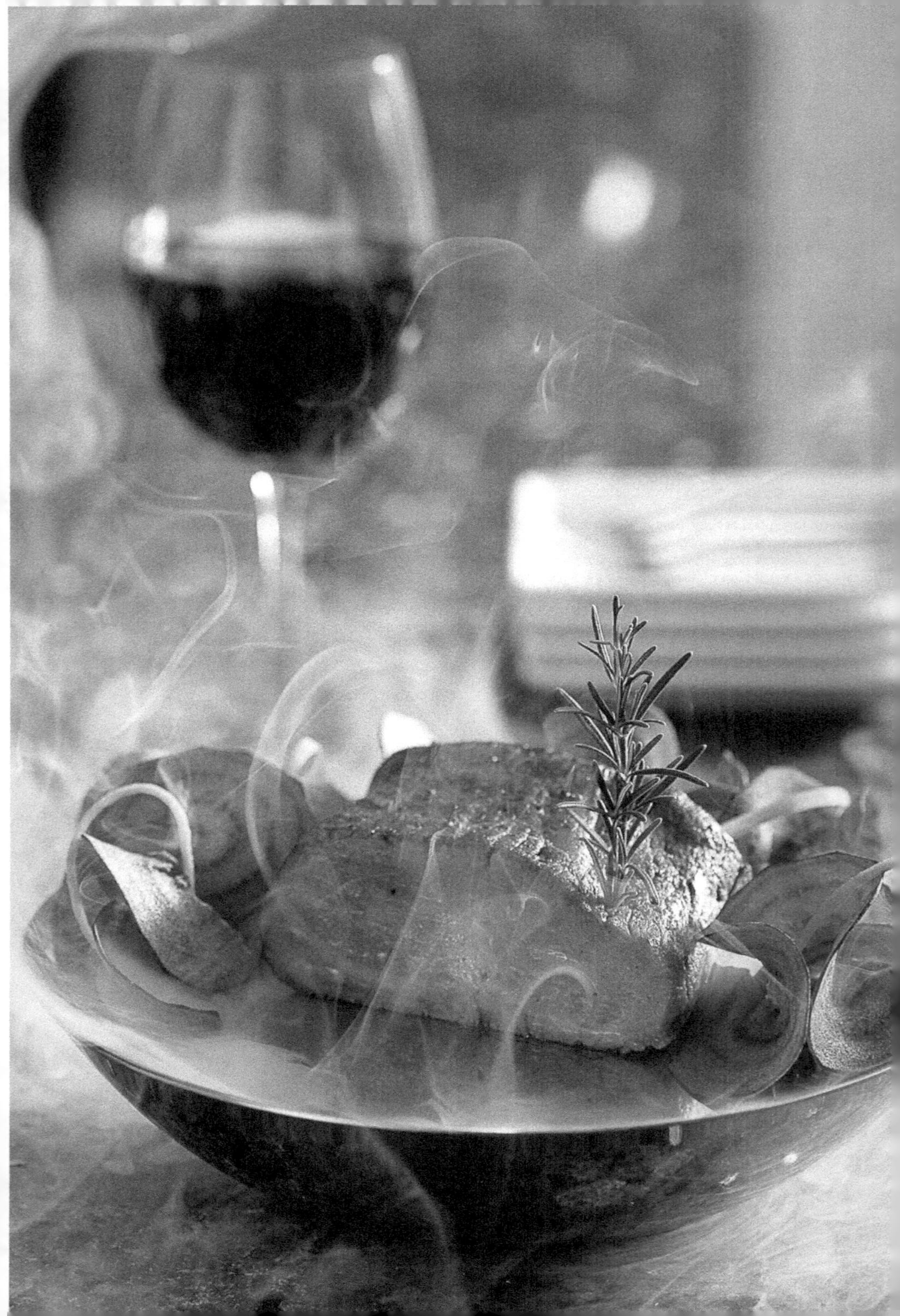

CHAPTER 13

FINANCIAL MANAGEMENT

"The problem isn't the problem. It's your attitude about the problem that's the problem. Do you understand?"

Captain Jack Sparrow

CASH FLOW

Cash flow is King! Positive cash flow results in a healthy business. Negative cash flow can lead to bankruptcy. Approximately 90% of small businesses in South Africa fail in their first year. The two main reasons being poor management and insufficient finance. Most people who start their own business seriously underestimate how much working capital they need, to their detriment. Of the remaining 10% who make it through their first year approximately 90% close within the first three years. Poor cash flow is one of the main causes of businesses failing.

A major contributor to poor cash flow is unrealistic drawings from a business. In other words, the owner of a business draws more money from the business than the business is able to sustain. Being unrealistic about the amount of money you draw from your business progressively erodes cash flow as the working capital in the business can no longer sustain the operating costs of the business. It takes time to reap the rewards from starting your own business. This is something that you should prepare yourself for.

Positive cash flow is when there is more actual money coming into a business than going out. Negative cash flow is when there is more money going out than in, leading to debt.

I say 'actual money' above as credit extended to a client is not actual money until the client pays. Photographers are often forced to extend unsecured credit to clients. In the magazine publishing industry in South Africa many magazines only pay the photographer in the month in which the story is used.

Considering that many titles work three months in advance this means that photographers are forced to extend the publisher 120 days unsecured credit. The magazines use their suppliers, including photographers, to fund the cost of publishing the magazine, only paying their suppliers once they receive the money for that edition. Whilst this ensures good cash flow for the publisher, it results in negative cash flow for photographers as photographers have to pay their overheads and cost of sales (their suppliers) before they receive payment from the publisher. This means that editorial photographers are often carrying four months of costs before being paid. The costs accumulate the busier the photographer is, adversely affecting the photographer's cash flow. It doesn't help having large sums of money on your books as credit extended to clients if you can't pay your immediate bills.

Once the cycle is rolling and the photographer has sufficient working capital to fund their clients the situation is manageable, until clients don't pay their invoices on time. Delayed payments cause the implosion of the photographers finances as they are normally already stretched too thin. The excuses for late payments are priceless, providing comic relief in otherwise exceptionally stressful times.

Good business practice dictates healthy, positive cash flow. Most photographers do not have large amounts of working capital backing their businesses and need to ensure that their terms of payment are as short as possible, with COD (cash on delivery) the preferred option.

It is always a good idea to secure a deposit for a job before starting it as the deposit assists with the operating costs of the job, assisting with cash flow. The size of the deposit is relative to the job. Wedding photographers tend to take large deposits up front, to confirm a booking, whilst advertising agencies tend to pay smaller deposits. I've never heard of a magazine paying a deposit to a photographer in South Africa.

CASH FLOW FORECAST

A cash flow forecast is a financial spread sheet that shows the cash flowing into and out of a business, over a period of time. It is an essential financial management tool used to establish budgets and targets and to monitor performance.

Photographers tend to be creative people who tend not to be administratively strong. A good book keeper is worth their weight in gold as they can help you with basic financial management.

Ensuring your book keeper has all the invoices, receipts and bank statements they need from you by the 3rd of the following month helps them to provide you with up to date management accounts by the 15th of that month. This simple, financial management practice means that you have a two week old historical financial picture of your business that you can take decisive action on quickly if need be.

By going through your cash flow forecast with your book keeper on a monthly basis you are able to plan your finances effectively and make provision for lean times ahead of time.

BANK ACCOUNT/SALARY

Understanding that your photography business is a business it needs it's own separate bank account. This may sound obvious but it's amazing how many people don't do this. Many photographers trade through their personal bank account. Determine the net salary you would like to draw (within reason) and draw it, on the same day of the month, every month, paying it across to your personal account from your business account. This helps with a number of things. First, it provides a financial history of your salary that you can use when applying for credit, such as a property bond. Second, it forces you not to spend 'surplus' money, leaving it in your business account to build up working capital. It's essential to do this as at some stage you will go through a quiet time during which you will need the working capital to cover your salary, amongst other things. Ensure all client payments are paid into your business account and pay all of your business expenses from your business account, completely separating your business and personal finances. This simplifies book keeping and taxation.

DEPRECIATION

Depreciation is one of the reasons why a business may appear profitable at first glance but on closer examination isn't. Assets wear out and need to be replaced. Depreciation is the term used to describe the way in which assets lose value over a period of time and is a reminder that they need to be replaced. Most photographic items depreciate over a period of three years. Cameras, lenses, lights etc wear out with use. The busier you are, the quicker they wear out. During the depreciation period you need to make financial provision for the replacement of the items. Many photographers remain trapped in the debt cycle as they borrow money to buy equipment, pay it off and then have to borrow money again to replace it as it wears out because they are not charging enough to be able to make provision for the equipments replacement (depreciation).

THE COST OF DEBT

Whilst most photographers extend their clients unsecured credit, very few suppliers extend it to photographers as it is bad business practice. The contracts we sign with banks, mobile phone companies and other suppliers are evidence of this. Before extending a client credit the client should complete a credit application form involving a background credit check.

I was once represented by an agent who secured a client for me who failed to pay their invoices. On handing them over for debt collection it came out that they had closed their previous business due to bankruptcy and started a new one, repeating their previous behaviour. The stress caused by this could have been avoided had the agent done a credit check before extending them credit.

The reality of debt is that it costs more than it's worth. Interest on debt costs approximately double what the interest on investments yield. Using your credit card or overdraft to bankroll a client costs you money and again, whilst it is good for their business, it is not good for yours. If you are in the fortunate position of having sufficient working capital to not use debt to finance jobs then the return on your investment into that job should exceed that of the return offered by another financial investment, otherwise is it worth doing at all?

The reality is, if you are unable to service your debt, your creditors will collect the money due to them, one way or another.

There are a number of finance options available to small businesses from overdrafts to credit cards, loans and factoring of invoices.

THE DEBT TRAP

South Africa is a debt society. The majority of the working population are caught in the debt trap. It's been said that in most South African families if the bread winner was to lose their job the family would be bankrupt within a month as they do not have the financial reserves to continue repaying their debt.

Borrowing money from financial institutions is risky. The interest charged often exceeds the potential financial return from the employed capital. This results in negative cash flow, often leading to the bankruptcy of the business.

Good financial management can prevent this. The danger of debt is in not being able to service it. Many people take loans to repay loans, 'Pinching from Peter to pay Paul', using an overdraft to pay their credit card as an example, ensnaring themselves in the debt trap. It is incredibly difficult to get out of the debt trap once caught in it as the only way out is to stop borrowing, lower your level of living and pay your debt as quickly as possible. The interest on debt accumulates quickly, making debt sometimes appear to be insurmountable.

Good financial management practices help to prevent this from happening, analysing the cost of debt verses the potential returns generated. A good accountant can assist you with this. The saying, "Wisdom comes from the council of many," applies. Think long and hard before borrowing money. Consult with your accountant and anyone else who's business opinion you respect before rushing into debt.

There are often alternative ways of doing what it is you want to do with less risk.

Some of the ways of avoiding the debt trap and improving your cash flow are:

- Keep your overheads down. Often the things we think are necessities aren't.
- Avoid credit terms. Use COD payment terms as much as possible, preferably securing a deposit before starting the job. Bad debts or invoices paid late can cripple your cash flow and possibly bankrupt your business.
- Debt collection. Follow up on invoices. A well timed phone call can make a big difference.

Your book keeper can do this for you. Be nice to your clients creditors clerk.

- Supplier payment terms. Use supplier payment terms to help your cash flow. If your suppliers allow you 30 days payment terms you have room to breathe. Alternatively negotiate discounts for COD payments to your suppliers.
- Keep stock levels to a minimum. Stock is working capital that is tied up. It costs money to buy and store and the money is only released when it is sold. Stock can be damaged or stolen, further negatively affecting cash flow.

FINANCIAL STATEMENTS

Financial statements are pictures of the financial state of your business and can tell you, at a glance, if your business is profitable or not.

The financial statements most commonly used in small businesses are:

- Cash Flow Statement - records the actual cash flowing into and out of your business, over a period of time, usually a month or a year.
- Income Statement, (Profit and Loss) - shows how profitable a business is by recording the income and expenses over a period, usually a month or year.
- Balance Sheet - records the financial position of a business at a particular point in time by comparing the assets (what the business owns) with the liabilities (what the business owes) and

the equity (finance received from the owner). A=E+L and should always balance.

Whilst financial statements tend to be historical (they tell you what has already happened in the business), they can also be used for budgeting or forecasting. By looking at the business's financial history, certain patterns emerge that become predictable, such as seasonal fluctuations in income and expenditure. This, coupled with your knowledge of your business, help to predict what may happen in the near future, giving you time to make the necessary adjustments to prevent negative scenarios.

TAXATION

Two things in life are certain. We will die and we will be taxed. Whilst many people pay tax grudgingly, we nevertheless must pay tax. Tax avoidance is legal. Tax evasion is not. A good Tax Practitioner knows the difference and can advise you accordingly.

If you are trading as a Sole Proprietor you need to register as a Provisional Tax Payer with the South African Revenue Service (SARS). Once you have registered, you need to submit 2-3 provisional tax returns per year. Whilst you can do this yourself through e filing, it is a good idea to hire a tax practitioner to calculate your tax due for you as they will know what expenses you can legitimately claim back. The higher your business expenses in relation to your income the less tax you pay. Standard provisional tax deducted by your clients is 25%.

If you employ people in your business you need to register for PAYE (Pay As You Earn) income tax, SDL (Skills Development Levy) and UIF (Unemployment Insurance Fund), deduct the applicable amounts from their salaries/wages and pay it across to the SARS. Your accountant can help you with this.

VAT

Regardless of the nature of the registration of your business, you can choose whether you want to register for VAT or not if your turnover is less than 1 million, but more than fifty-five thousand rand per year. There are pros and cons for registering, or not, that you should consult your accountant about. If you do choose to register for VAT remember that you need to pay VAT across to the SARS every four months. It's a good idea to have a 'VAT control' savings account that you pay the VAT that you charge into, that you can then pay VAT across to the SARS when you need to. At the very least you will earn some interest on the money before paying it across to the SARS.

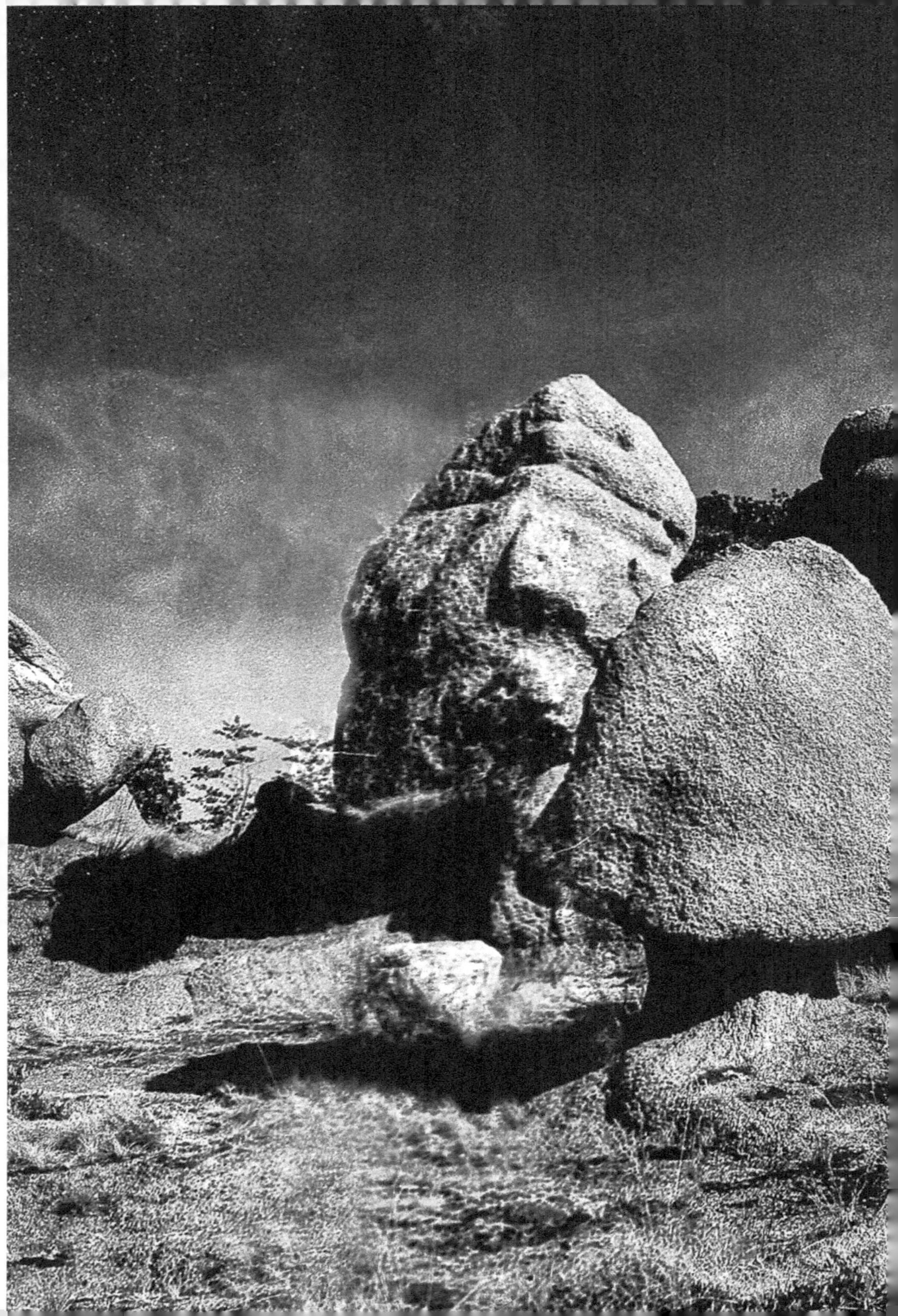

CHAPTER 14

PROFESSIONAL SUPPORT SERVICES

"Talent wins games, but teamwork and intelligence wins championships."

Michael Jordan

To be successful in business we need to be realistic about our strengths and weaknesses. Knowing that you are not administratively strong and still trying to do your own books to try to save money is not a good idea. It will probably lead to you losing money without realising it.

Different people specialise in different fields. Just as you specialise in photography, other people specialise in their chosen career. The professional support services you are likely to need are:

BOOK KEEPER

Apart from your bank manager your book keeper is your best friend in business, as long as they do their job properly. A book keeper records the day to day transactions of a business within the financial management framework of the business. From capturing petty cash expenses to bank statements a book keeper ensures that the income and expenses of a business are captured correctly, transferring the captured information to financial statements. A book keeper normally only works up to Cash Flow Statement and Income Statement levels. Your book keeper can compile your monthly books that you can use for the financial management of your business.

ACCOUNTANT

An accountant is a professionally qualified person with a university degree in accounting, registered with a professional body like the Institute of Chartered

Accountants of South Africa. An accountant checks and adjusts the financial statements to the final Balance Sheet and normally completes the financial year end of the business. Accountants ensure that the business complies with all the required financial legal requirements. It is not normally necessary to meet with your accountant on a monthly basis in a small business unless you need their advice on financial or business strategy.

AUDITOR

Auditors conduct strictly regulated examinations of businesses to determine the accuracy and reliability of a business's financial statements. It is not legally required for Sole Proprietors, Partnerships or Close Corporations (ccs) to be audited. Companies are legally required to be audited on an annual basis except for companies with a turnover of less than 5 million rand who may conduct voluntary audits but are not legally required to do so. The auditing process is an expensive one but the advantage of being audited is that institutions accept the business's financial statements as being a correct and true reflection of the business, that helps when trying to secure finance or sell shares in the business.

ATTORNEY

Attorneys, or lawyers, are professionally qualified people, with a university degree, registered with a professional body like the Cape Law Society, who specialise in law. Attorneys specialise in many different fields of law from criminal to commercial, intellectual property and family law. It's essential to match an attorney's specialisation with your needs. It doesn't help consulting an attorney who specialises in family law about intellectual property. Whilst attorneys are expensive, they will often offer an initial consultation for free that assists with clarifying what action you should take in a particular matter.

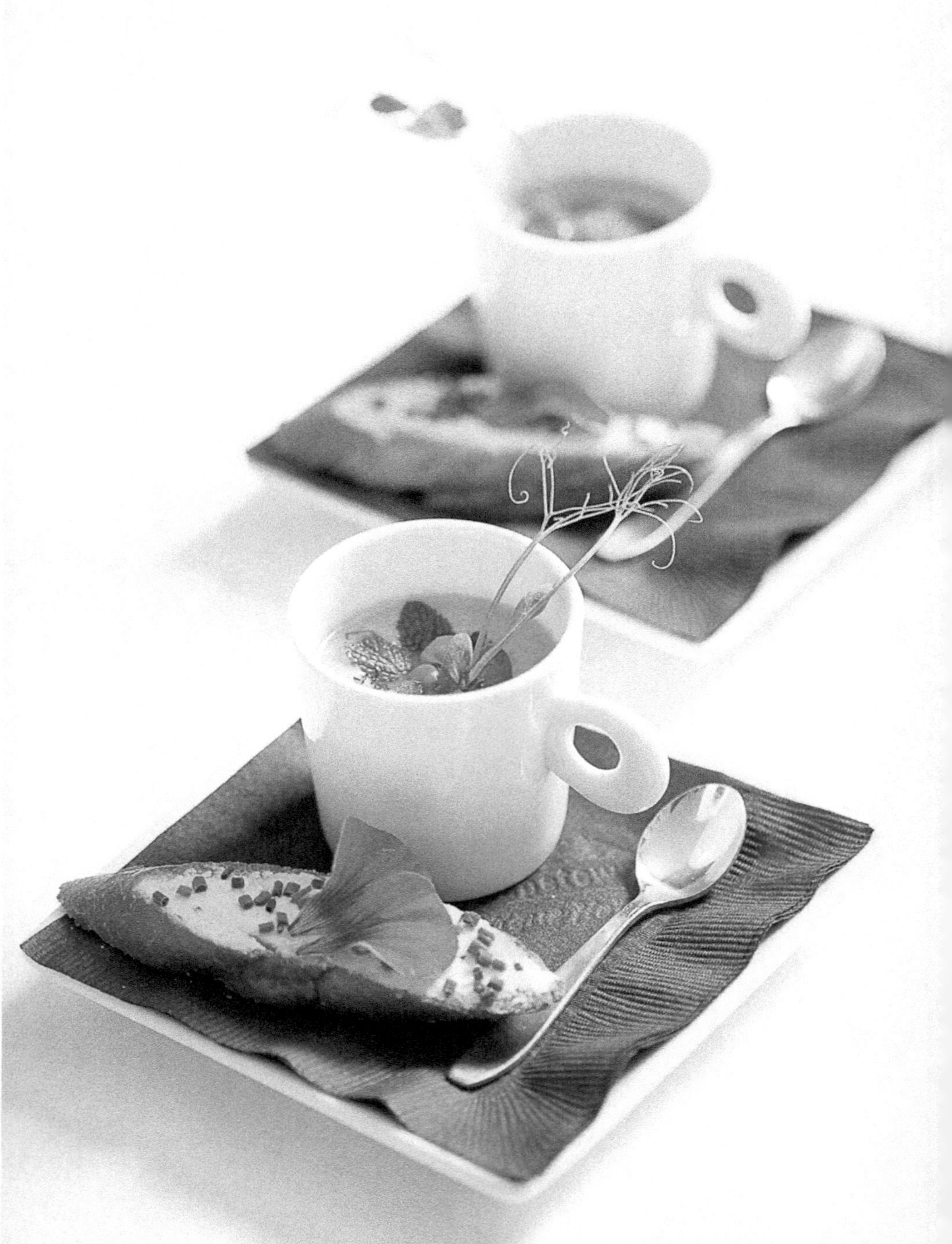

CHAPTER 15

MARKETING

"Decide the market you want to tap, then produce the work that will win them over, shine and they will follow."

Michael J. Lewis

In business terms the act of creating imagery as a photographer is referred to as 'production'. The financial management of the business is referred to as 'administration'. The third leg of a business is 'sales and marketing'. Without sales and marketing there can be no production or administration. Production is driven by demand that is created by sales and marketing.

You can fulfil certain basic marketing functions yourself as a photographer but there will come a point at which you are better off hiring someone else to market your business for you, to free yourself up to do what you do best - creating images. Many photographers take on an agent to do this for them. There are pros and cons for taking on an agent dealt with later in this chapter.

At the very least you need the following:

BUSINESS CARD

Your business card needs to clearly display your name, your business name, your business registration number (if registered), your contact details including your phone number, fax number, e mail and web site address and your logo if you have one. Remember that photography is a creative field and your business card should reflect this. Your business card is your primary marketing tool and you should give it out to everyone you come into contact with who may be a potential client.

LETTER HEAD

Your letter head should display the same details as your business card, as well as your address and the names of the partners/members/directors of your business. All of your business correspondence should be on your business letterhead, including your cost estimates and invoices, unless using a specialised template for those.

WEB SITE

Your web site is your most important marketing tool as it is your online portfolio and should be a true reflection of your work, should be updated frequently and must have your contact details clearly displayed. Key words are important as if a potential client is searching the internet for a photographer you want them to find your site. Your keywords should include your name, your products and services and your location. It is well worth learning the basics of SEO (Search Engine Optimisation) to improve your search rankings. Considering that your web site is your most important marketing tool it is where the bulk of your marketing budget should be focussed. A professionally designed photographers web site costs approximately R25 000,00. Your web site needs to be updated regularly with your new work so it is advisable to ensure that it has 'user login' functionality so that you or your assistant can update it cost effectively.

PORTFOLIO

Apart from your web site you also need a physical portfolio. This can be presented as a 'coffee table book' (photo book), or on a tablet like an iPad, or using a photographic portfolio book with sleeves that you can slide photographs and tear sheets from published jobs into. The golden rule of marketing as a photographer is PORTFOLIO, PORTFOLIO, PORTFOLIO. Your portfolio showcases your work and talent as a photographer and clients will choose you, or not, based on the strength of your portfolio. Again, you are in a creative field and the presentation of your portfolio should reflect this. Once you have a lead for a potential job you will be required to present your portfolio when meeting with the client. This is your opportunity to sell your services in a confident way that persuades the client to use you, and not one of the other photographers they have seen or are about to see.

ADVERTISING

There are many forms of advertising. As a wedding photographer it's a good idea to advertise your services in local newspapers, through wedding planners and on the internet using targetable advertising like Google Ads or Facebook Ads. As a commercial photographer you should advertise in mediums that reach your target market. It's important to do your market research to find out who the actual person is who commissions photographers in a company you would like to shoot for and to target your advertising at them. Email marketing campaigns are similar to distributing fliers, have a very low readership and an even lower engagement. There are more effective ways of reaching your target market that a marketing specialist can advise you of.

PHOTO COMPETITIONS

Photo competitions are an excellent way to showcase your work and hopefully win an award, and the prestige that accompanies it. There are many international photo competitions every year, some more prestigious than others. Always read the terms and conditions of photo competitions as some are thinly disguised photo libraries claiming the copyright, or right to sub-license your images, as part of the terms and conditions of entry. If you enter your images, you're agreeing to the terms. The Artists Bill of Rights Campaign is an organisation that tackles dodgy competitions. You can report these competitions to them through their web site www.artists-bill-of-rights.org. Reputable organisers of photo competitions can use the Artists Bill of Rights logo in their marketing and information after registering with the organisation.

CORPORATE IDENTITY

Regardless of the marketing tools you need it is essential to develop your own, unique, unified corporate identity, that will be applied to all of your marketing material. Photography is a creative field and your corporate identity should reflect this. If you are not a trained graphic designer yourself then it's a good idea to commission one to develop your corporate identity.

Once your designer has designed a logo that you feel represents you and your core philosophies, and chosen your corporate colours and fonts, these need to be applied across ALL of your corporate material, from your business cards to compliment slips, letter heads, email signature, web site and other online presence. A unique, unified corporate identity becomes easily recognisable helping to build your brand and re-enforce your marketing message.

SOCIAL MEDIA

Social media is the latest and greatest thing right now but is it all it appears to be? As the various platforms attract investors interest they change to become more profitable.

Some of the social media platforms use terms and conditions like the following:

> *XXX does not claim ownership of any Content that you post on or through the Service. Instead, you hereby grant to XXX a non-exclusive, fully paid and royalty-free, transferable, sub-licensable, worldwide license to use the Content that you post on or through the Service.*

The license for use that you are agreeing to by using the service is broad and in effect empowers them to sub-license your content, without paying royalties to you. Furthermore they hold you responsible and liable for any claims arising out of the use of your content with clauses like:

> *You represent and warrant that: (i) you own the Content posted by you on or through the Service or otherwise have the right to grant the rights and licenses set forth in these Terms of Use; (ii) the posting and use of your Content on or through the Service does not violate, misappropriate or infringe*

on the rights of any third party, including, without limitation, privacy rights, publicity rights, copyrights, trademark and/or other intellectual property rights; (iii) you agree to pay for all royalties, fees, and any other monies owed by reason of Content you post on or through the Service; and (iv) you have the legal right and capacity to enter into these Terms of Use in your jurisdiction.

Social media is a powerful marketing tool, but should be used carefully. By uploading your images to your own web site, that you control the terms and conditions for use of, and posting the link (URL) onto social networks for publicity, is one way of overcoming this. The 'content' you are posting is the link itself and not your images.

The American Society of Media Photographers (www.asmp.org) publishes updated information about social media networks and the changes to their terms and conditions.

AGENTS

As with every other field there are good and bad photographic agents. Choosing your agent is personal as you are choosing a person to represent you the way that you want to be represented. Not only must your agent advertise and market you to secure work, they must also manage the production of the jobs they bring you and administer them too, including invoicing and collection of payment.

There is a lot of trust involved in being represented by an agent as they handle the negotiations around money. They are paid on a commission only basis, normally between 20-25% of your BUR as well as buyouts. Buyouts are often requested some time after a job has been completed and these negotiations take place between the client and the agent, without your knowledge, unless your agent involves you in the process, which they should. There have been a number of cases in South Africa in which an agent has charged a client usage, taken the money and not paid it across to the photographer.

The relationship between a photographer and his/her agent should be in writing, in a contract. To date I have been represented by three different agents in my career, none of them ending well. One of the agents I was represented by referred to herself as *'the best agent in Cape Town'*. When I asked about a written agreement she told me that she *'doesn't do contracts'*. I was young and naive and didn't insist on one at the time, thinking that she was honest and trustworthy. Later, I realised that she was not being open and honest with me and asked her for supporting documentation for jobs, that she refused to supply, telling me that her computer crashed, she didn't have backups and didn't have paper copies of the documents on file. A little later she then sent me an invoice that was very clearly not the invoice sent to the client. Needless to say our relationship did not end well. It recently came out that she had been charging clients usage and not paying it across to a photographer she represented, keeping the money for herself. Whilst the photographer has left her he is apparently still trying to get his money from her. This is clearly an example of a dishonest agent to be avoided. Not all agents are dishonest.

The Association of Photographers (AOP) has a downloadable photographer/agent agreement that you can use as a base agreement with your agent and customise it to your needs if necessary. This agreement clearly defines the roles and responsibilities of the relationship and can be used as a basis for legal action if necessary.

To get a feel for an agent, you can contact the artists already represented by him/her to determine how the agent operates, if the artists receive the money due to them when it's due and if the agent is trustworthy or not. Remember that agents receive many requests from photographers to represent them and they are not obliged to represent you in any way. The relationship is based on mutual financial benefit.

The advantage of being represented by a good, honest photographic agent is that they free you up to focus on what you do best, whilst they take care of your marketing, production and billing. Your agent should have an 'open books' policy with you, allowing you to investigate the documentation around your jobs at any time. It is advisable to never sign a power of attorney with your agent as this empowers them to sign documentation on your behalf. By insisting on signing all agreements yourself, especially licensing agreements, you will have more insight into, and control over, your jobs.

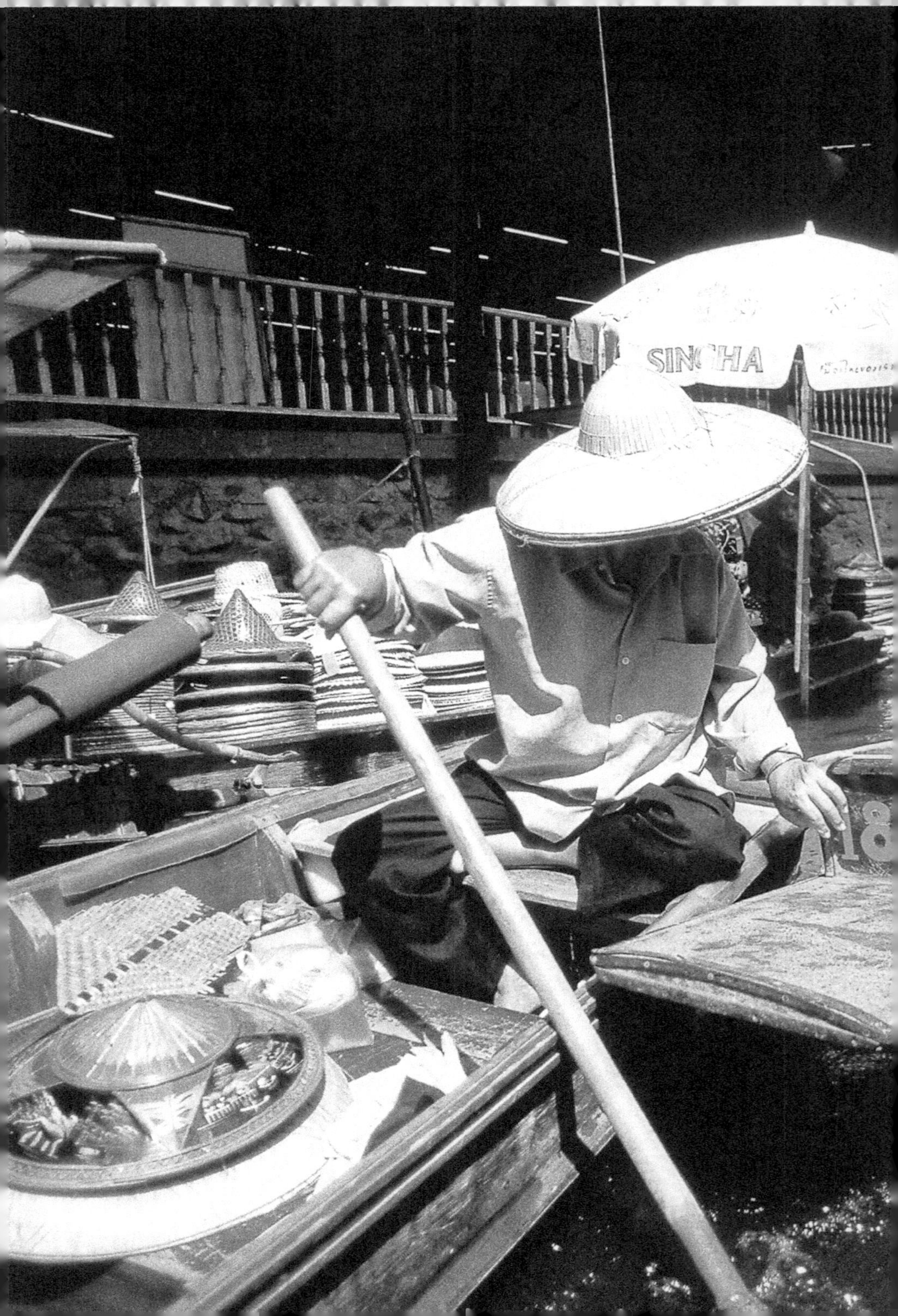
SINGHA
18

CHAPTER 16

PRODUCTION

"Everyone has a photographic memory, but not everyone has film."

Anonymous

Regardless of the level or type of photography you do you will need to do a certain level of production management.

Management is about planning, organising, leading and controlling. Managers plan the work, organise the resources, lead the people and control the result.

Advertising assignments tend to require the most production management, although this is not always the case. Every assignment should start with a written brief. The brief specifies the requirements and the details of the job. It is common for a photographer to employ a producer or production manager to manage the job for them so that they can focus on creating incredible images without worrying about logistical details.

Costing a brief takes time and energy. Resources have to be sourced, quotations obtained from suppliers and the work planned to determine its full scope before the completed estimate can be submitted to the client. Clients do not normally pay for the preparation of cost estimates, photographers do this at their own risk.

Once you have been awarded the job the next phase is preproduction, the preparation of the job for production. All aspects of production are chargeable, not just the actual shoot days. Preproduction involves the following:

- Attendance of meetings and briefings
- Location scouting, light checks and optioning selected locations
- Obtaining required permits
- Model casting and optioning selected models

- Sourcing and optioning props
- Optioning transport
- Optioning accommodation
- Optioning crew
- Optioning equipment

Once production starts options are converted to bookings and the work starts.

A useful management tool is to draw up a production schedule. This is a plan, or program of the entire production and includes information like the activities per day, models, locations, props, equipment as well as crew required for that day. The layout needs to be clear and simple to understand. This is issued to everyone on set along with a call sheet. A call sheet is a list of every person on set's names, functions and contact details.

At the end of the production the job needs to be reconciled to ensure that it can be correctly billed to the client. During the job, it is the producer's job to ensure that the job is brought in within budget. Any item not allowed for in the cost estimate becomes an 'extra' item and should be agreed with the client on set before proceeding. The reconciliation at the end of the job is a financial spreadsheet that lists the actual costs of the job. The final invoice is prepared from the reconciliation.

It is advisable to secure a deposit from the client to cover production expenses. Whilst the photographer's fee can be invoiced once the finished artworks have been delivered the client should carry the cost of production by paying the production costs up front.

BOOKING MODELS

Model agencies work according to a strict set of guidelines. The booking system works as follows:

- 2nd Option - Another client holds a first option but if they don't book the model, you can.
- 1st Option - You have the model and must either confirm or release the option a minimum of 24 hours before.
- Weather booking - The model is booked but if the weather is bad you can roll over to another day. The model will make a weather call in the morning and it is the photographer's responsibility to decide whether or not to go ahead. The weather day is not charged for by the model agency, if unable to shoot due to undesirable weather. Once the model arrives they must be paid for, regardless of whether the shoot takes place or not.
- Booking - The model is booked, irrespective of weather, and must be paid for.

WORKING HOURS

The working hours for models are measured from the 'call time' (the time the model is required to arrive) to 'last shot' (the time the last shot finishes). Travel time for distances of more than 60 km is charged for with a full day's travel charged at 50% of the day rate, per day.

According to the National Association of Model Agencies (NAMA)[8]:

- A local full day is 9 hours that includes one hour for lunch with a half day of 4 hours.
- An international full day is 11 hours that includes one hour for lunch with a half day of 5 hours.
- Night shoots are based on 10 hours, regardless of the call time, with 150% of the day rate charged for the first night for international shoots.
- A Call Back (from a casting) may not exceed 2 consecutive hours. Thereafter 15% of the Day Rate per hour or part thereof for local and 10% of the Day Rate per hour or part thereof for international shoots is charged.
- The first 2 hours for fittings is free, thereafter R250 per hour or part thereof for Local and 10% of the Day Rate per hour or part thereof for International shoots is charged.
- Overtime is charged at 15% of the Day Rate per hour or part thereof for the first 4 hours for local shoots, then 20% per hour or part thereof over 4 hours. International shoots are 10% of the Day Rate per hour or part thereof.
- A Rejection Fee of 100% of the Day Rate is charged for completed shoots that are rejected by the client.

---

[8] National Association of Model Agencies www.nama.co.za

- 150% of the Day Rate is charged for topless modelling with double the Day Rate (200%) for nude modelling.

The NAMA guidelines are not legislated and model agencies tend to vary from the guidelines. It's essential to clarify the details with the specific model agency you deal with to ensure you have the correct applicable terms when you compile your Cost Estimate.

CHILD MODELS

The use of children as models is governed by the *Basic Conditions of Employment Act, No. 75 of 1997, Sectorial Determination 10: Children in the Performance of Advertising, Artistic, and Cultural Activities, South Africa,* applicable to children under 15 years of age.

The Sectorial Determination 10 is a clear set of legal requirements for working with children and covers topics like permits, working hours, night work, rest periods, food and refreshments and penalties, amongst others.

The permitted maximum number of working hours is governed by the child's age and is found in Part D:

PART D: HOURS OF WORK

8 HOURS OF WORK

(1) For purposes of this Determination the maximum permissible hours of work are:

a) in respect of a child aged over ten years, four hours a day;

b) in respect of a child of ten years or younger, three hours a day.

2) An employer may not require or permit a child to work for longer than the maximum permissible hours of work.

3) An employer may not require or permit a child to be present at the workplace on any day for more than-

a) ten hours, in the case of a child aged over ten years;

b) eight hours, in the case of a child aged older than five years but not older than ten years;

c) six hours, in the case of a child aged younger than five years.

4) No employer may force a child to perform when the child is not ready or fit to do so.

ATA CARNET

When traveling outside of your country it is advisable to use an ATA Carnet for your equipment. A Carnet or ATA Carnet (pronounced kar-nay) is an international customs and export-import document. It is used to clear customs without paying duties and import taxes on merchandise that will be exported within 12 months

The carnet forms are available from your local Chamber of Commerce and requires a substantial deposit. Most first world and some third world countries use the carnet system.

According to the South African Chamber of Commerce and Industry web site www.sacci.org.za[9] as at the 16th September 2015 (please check the web site for updated rates):

The cost of an ATA Carnet is:

Issuing Fee

- *R3,200.00 for the value of goods up to R100,000.00*
- *R4,800.00 for the value of goods over R100,000.00*
- *Deposit or Guarantee Letter: 50% of the total value of the goods.*
- *25% of the total value of the goods for the Carnets to Botswana, Lesotho, Namibia & Swaziland (BLNS)*
- *Minimum Deposit is R5,000.00*

---

[9] http://www.sacci.org.za/index.php?option=com_content&view=article&id=44&Itemized=53

Carnet holders are not required to post securities with customs. Carnets simplify customs border crossing and cut red tape by allowing importers and exporters to use a single document for all customs formalities.[10]

Some countries that do not use the carnet system require a deposit to be paid at the point of entry, that is refunded on leaving the country. The deposit can be up to 100% of the value of the equipment, that must be paid at the point of entry. This can become a cash flow nightmare if you don't make allowance for it and your working capital for your job is tied up in the deposit.

It's a good idea to keep a few copies of an itemised list of your equipment, with serial numbers, with you when traveling.

POST PRODUCTION

Post production occurs once the actual shoot is finished. Post production involves the selection, correction and processing out of the images created. Once the final images have been selected for use they are sent in for retouching and then supplied to the client as finished artworks. The retouching of images is a specialist field in itself. Using professional retouchers not only improves the quality of the finished artwork but also tends to save time as professional retouchers tend to work a lot quicker than most photographers attempting to retouch their own work.

---

[10] http://www.sacci.org.za/index.php?option=com_content&view=article&id=41&Itemized=50

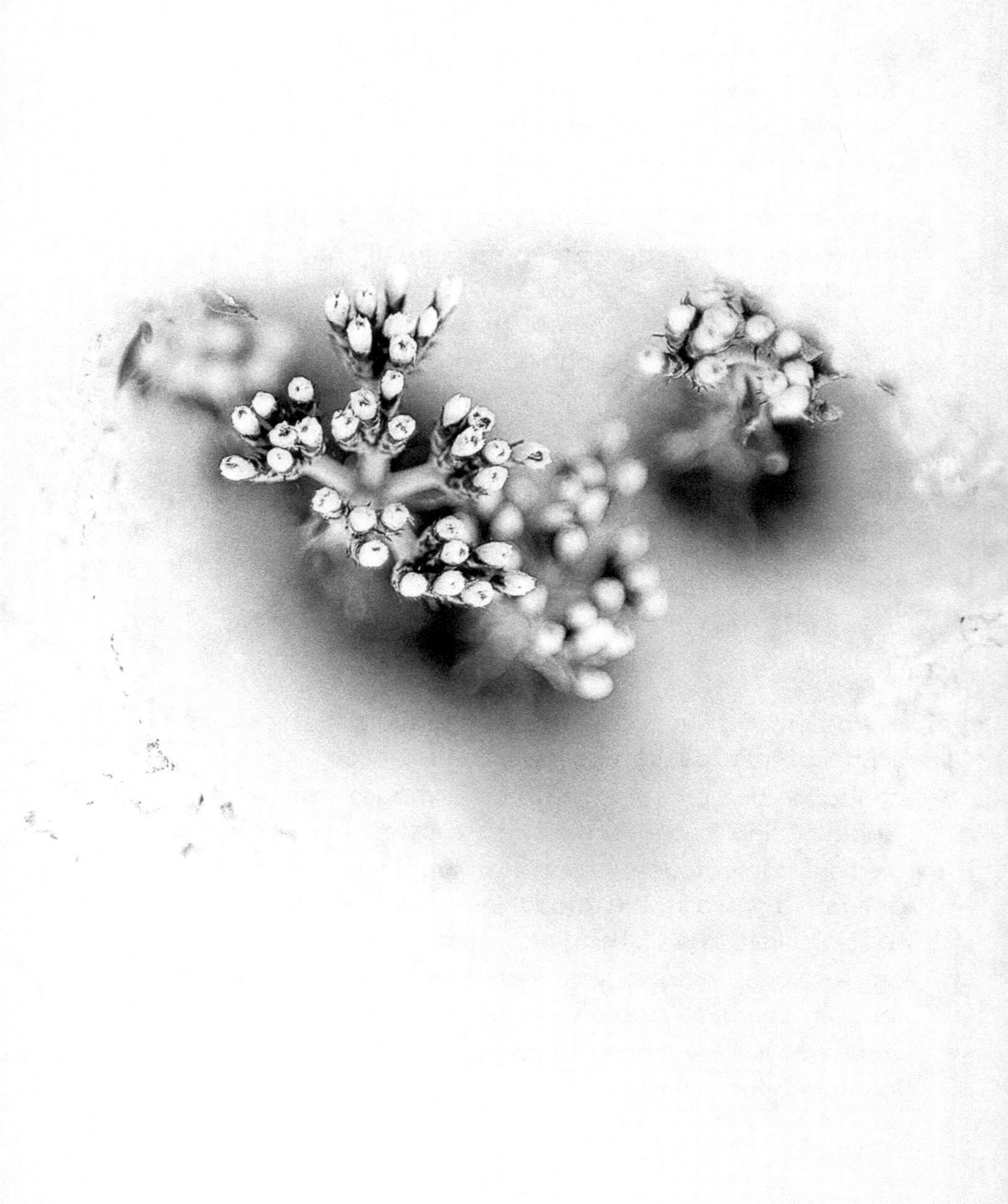

CHAPTER 17

FROM ZERO TO HERO

"Photography is a love affair with life."

Burk Uzzle

Congratulations, you've completed your studies and you've taken the leap of faith to go into the industry. The big question remaining is, 'Where to from here?'

There are a number of entry points into the photographic industry.

COMMERCIAL PHOTOGRAPHY

There is a global industry accepted standard for entering Commercial Photography and that is to start by assisting an established photographer.

Choose the photographer you assist carefully. Try to assist a photographer who specialises in the genre that interests you the most.

Assisting is not only about learning the technical aspects of photography but also, equally important, the business of photography. By assisting the right photographer you will make the industry contacts you will need when you go pro, as well as learn some of the do's and don'ts of doing business in the industry.

As an assistant your most employable traits will be punctuality, reliability, a 'can do' attitude and how well you make coffee. If you are consistently punctual; do what you are asked to do within the time frame allowed; are a well mannered, not 'in your face' person and make excellent coffee, chances are you'll be asked to come back.

Realistically you should assist for at least four years before going pro. This gives you the time to mature as a person and learn the ins and outs of the industry so that by the time you go pro you're ready, know the industry and are going in with your eyes open.

There are a few different kinds of assistants.

- First Assistant / Camera Assistant
- Second Assistant / Lighting Assistant
- Digital Assistant
- Runner / Driver

A first assistant is someone who is skilled enough to go pro but is putting in their last bit of time polishing their skills and knowledge. Most first assistants have started taking on small jobs of their own. The first assistant reports directly to the photographer and focusses on the overall production and camera requirements.

A second assistant is someone who is training to be a first assistant and reports to the first assistant. The second assistant tends to focus more on the setting up and taking down of lighting as well as other general tasks. Second assistants are often expected to drive the equipment vehicle.

A digital assistant works exclusively with the digital aspects of the shoot and reports directly to the photographer. He/she ensures that the camera is loaded correctly and is communicating with the computer on set. The digital assistant downloads, checks, processes out and backs up the entire shoot, normally while the photographer is shooting. A digital assistant may also be required to do some retouching of the images. Digital assistants are expected to know programs like Capture One Pro, Adobe Lightroom, Aperture, Adobe Bridge and Adobe Photoshop backwards.

A runner/driver is a general hand on set tasked with doing whatever they are asked to, and normally reports to the first assistant as well. A runner/driver is often training to become a second assistant.

Most assistants are employed on a freelance basis. In South Africa we rarely have the budgets to employ the above assistants and our first assistant is often required to do the jobs of the first, second and digital assistants.

An excellent place to learn a lot in a very short time is to assist on international shoots. This is a lot easier than it may seem. Local Stills Production Companies hire photographic assistants (first and second), digital assistants, production assistants, location scouts, runners and production managers on a freelance basis. The advantages of working on international shoots is that you earn more and work to an international standard that is quite different to the norm in South Africa.

The South African Association of Stills Producers (SAASP) has a list of local production companies on their web site http://www.saasp.co.za/

RETOUCHING

If you love Photoshop and spending hours behind the computer then retouching may be for you. Choose a successful retoucher/retouching business to approach.

Many of these businesses are already fully staffed and your only way in may be to work as an intern in the beginning. Considering that this may be your chosen career, interning for a few months is a worthwhile investment, to learn what you need to know to become a professional retoucher.

SUPPORT SERVICES

There are numerous support services in the photographic industry from equipment hire companies to location companies, photographic shops and print labs, all of which are potential employers of a keen, dedicated person with a basic knowledge of photography.

DOCUMENTARY PHOTOGRAPHY

Many newspapers and magazines employ in-house photographers. A number of publishing companies have in-house, fully equipped studios as well.

It can be very challenging making a living from documentary photography as a freelancer. A salaried, in-house position offers a more stable income with some job security. In-house job vacancies don't come up very often and your entry point may be to start out as a freelance contributor to meet the right people. Should an in-house position open up, you should have a better chance of securing the job if you are already known to the publication. Interning for media companies is also a great way to learn the ropes and get to know the right people.

SOCIAL PHOTOGRAPHY

One of the easiest points of entry into Professional Photography is Social Photography, photographing weddings, birthdays, corporate cocktail parties, etc. This type of photography requires some basic photography training and the rest is 'flash on camera' 'point and shoot', capturing the best moments possible, in the best way possible. This can be applied from your local area to Cruise Ships traveling around the world.

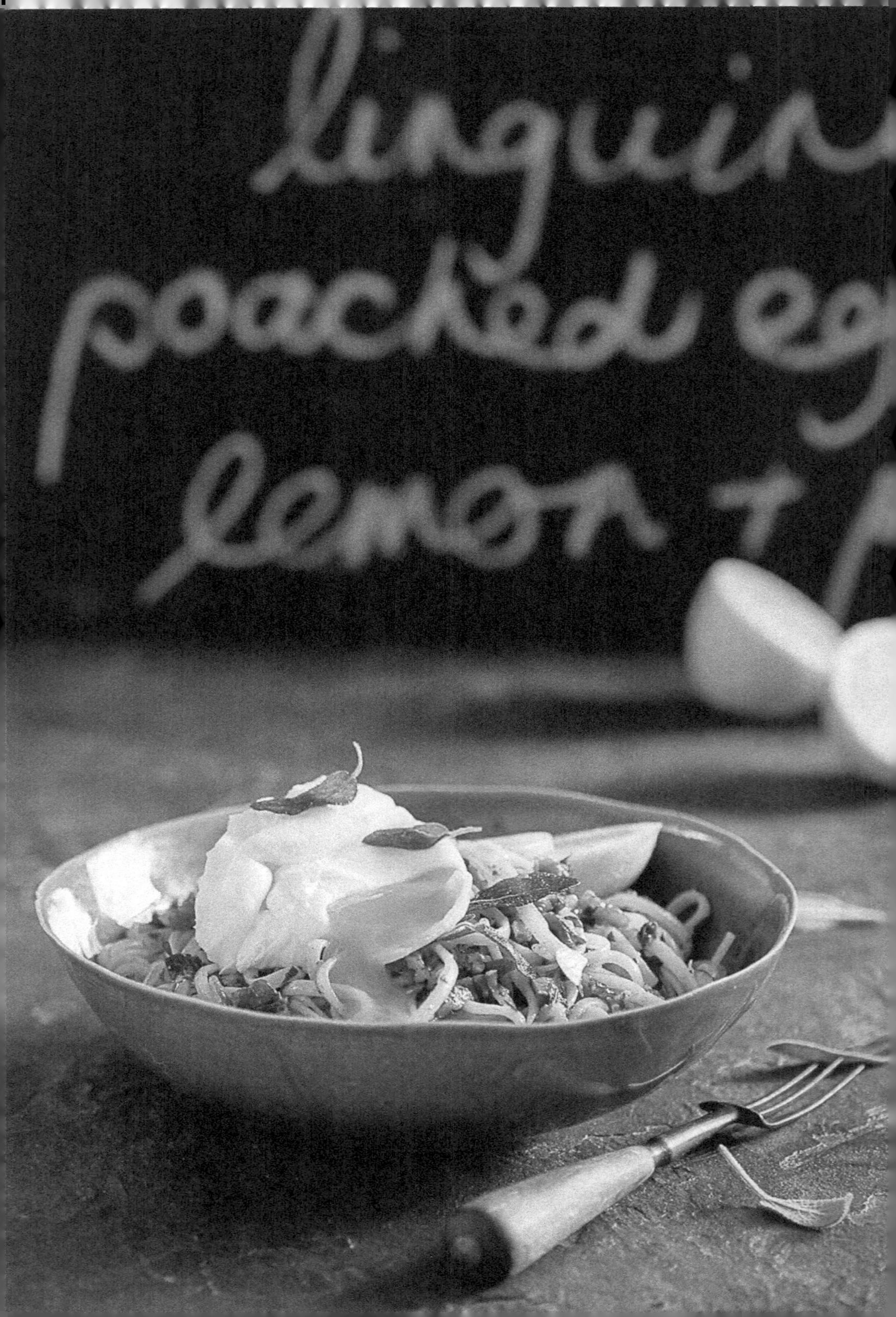
linguin
poached eg
lemon +

CHAPTER 18

WHERE TO FROM HERE?

"You need to find yourself a girl mate. Or perhaps the reason you practice three hours a day is that you already found one, and are otherwise incapable of wooing said strumpet. You're not a eunuch are you?"

Captain Jack Sparrow

Professional photography is a business. Whilst the products we sell are the physical manifestations of the creations of our minds, and our drive is our passion to create imagery, we cannot escape the fact that it is still a business.

One of the fundamental principles of a business is to make a profit. To have a financially sustainable and viable career as a professional photographer we must manage our businesses to be profitable. This sounds obvious but it never ceases to amaze me how many photographers businesses are running at a loss, which they are unaware of. The stigma of 'struggling photographers' can and should be changed. It starts with educating ourselves, and then educating our clients. Most clients are not unreasonable and if you explain costs to them clearly and coherently, they understand and accommodate them, within reason. The onus is on us to do that.

Remember that just because a potential client approaches you, it doesn't mean you have to work for them. If it doesn't make financial sense then I suggest you walk away. Why pay someone to work for them? You're better off investing your hard earned money into an investment account where you are at least likely to make a return on your investment.

SOURCES OF REFERENCE

PHOTOGRAPHY ASSOCIATIONS, SOCIETIES AND INFORMATION FORUMS

American Photographic Artists (APA) www.editorialphoto.com

Artists Bill of Rights Campaign www.artists-bill-of-rights.org

C21 www.c21.za.org

Exposed www.exposed.co.za

Photo District News www.pdnonline.com

Professional Photographer www.professionalphotographer.co.uk

Photo Shelter www.photoshelter.com

The American Society of Media Photographers (USA) www.asmp.org

The Association of Photographers (AOP) www.the-aop.org, 'Beyond the Lens' Rights, Ethics and Business Practice in Professional Photography

The Photographic Society of South Africa (PSSA) www.pssa.co.za

World Photography Organisation www.worldphoto.org

PRODUCTION RESOURCES

Commercial Producers Association of South Africa (CPASA) www.cpasa.tv for general production information and crew terms and conditions

National Association of Model Agencies (NAMA) www.nama.co.za for information on terms and conditions for models

South African Association of Stills Producers (SAASP) www.saasp.co.za for general stills production information

OTHER WEB SITES

Entrepreneur Magazine www.entrepreneurmag.co.za

Small Enterprise Development Agency www.seda.org.za

South African Business Plans www.sabusinessplans.co.za

The South African Chamber of Commerce and Industry www.sacci.org.za

BOOKS/BOOKLETS

'*A Basic Guide to the Law of Copyright*' 5th Edition, 2006 Dr Gernholtz Inc. Intellectual Property Attorneys by Dr Richard Gernholtz

'*Basic Guide to Intellectual Property Law*' Dr Gernholtz Inc. Intellectual Property Attorneys by Dr Richard Gernholtz, John Spicer and Otto C. Gernholtz

'*Beyond the Lens*' 3rd Edition 2003, published by The Association of Photographers Limited

'*Business Basics - A practical guide for small business owners*' by Standard Bank

'Dean and Dyer's Digest of Intellectual Property Law' by Oxford University Press, co-edited by Dr. Owen Dean

'Handbook of South African Copyright Law' by Dr. Owen Dean

'International Privacy, Publicity and Personality Laws' edited by Michael Henry

'Professional Business Practices in Photography' by the American Society of Media Photographers (www.asmp.org)

ABOUT THE AUTHOR

Deryck van Steenderen is an international commercial photographer who has shot prestigious advertising campaigns and editorial assignments for top agencies and magazines.

Deryck is passionate about the financial viability and sustainability of the photographic industry in South Africa and has lectured in 'Professional Practice' at top photography universities, colleges and schools throughout the country. He is an invited guest speaker on 'Professional Practice' and 'Copyright for Photographers' and spoke four years in a row at the Photo & Film Expo in Johannesburg.

Deryck's Grandfather and namesake, Dr. Deryck Humphriss, gave him his first camera, a Russian Zenit 35mm film camera, at the age of 15 and he's been shooting ever since. Initially Deryck was drawn to hard news photojournalism. At the age of 18 his reportage work on 'Life in Alexandra' was exhibited in the Union Buildings in Pretoria. At 22 his photographs of the Chris Hani riots in Cape Town sold internationally. Following the end of apartheid in South Africa Deryck left photojournalism for a career as a commercial photographer. He also works on personal fine art photography projects that exhibit internationally.

"To leave the world a bit better... to know that one life has breathed easier because you have lived. This is to have succeeded."

Ralph Waldo Emerson

www.ingramcontent.com/pod-product-compliance
Lightning Source LLC
Chambersburg PA
CBHW060839170526
45158CB00001B/187